IN SUPPORT OF
SAME-SEX MARRIAGE & GAY RIGHTS
IN AMERICA

THOMAS J. SCHUH

Note for Librarians: a cataloguing record for this book that includes Dewey Decimal Classification and US Library of Congress numbers is available from the Library and Archives of Canada. The complete cataloguing record can be obtained from their online database at:
www.collectionscanada.ca/amicus/index-e.html
ISBN 1-4120-4352-2

TRAFFORD

Offices in Canada, USA, Ireland, UK and Spain
This book was published *on-demand* in cooperation with Trafford Publishing. On-demand publishing is a unique process and service of making a book available for retail sale to the public taking advantage of on-demand manufacturing and Internet marketing. On-demand publishing includes promotions, retail sales, manufacturing, order fulfilment, accounting and collecting royalties on behalf of the author.
Book sales for North America and international:
Trafford Publishing, 6E–2333 Government St.,
Victoria, BC v8t 4p4 CANADA
phone 250 383 6864 (toll-free 1 888 232 4444)
fax 250 383 6804; email to orders@trafford.com
Book sales in Europe:
Trafford Publishing (uk) Ltd., Enterprise House, Wistaston Road Business Centre, Wistaston Road, Crewe, Cheshire cw2 7rp UNITED KINGDOM
phone 01270 251 396 (local rate 0845 230 9601)
facsimile 01270 254 983; orders.uk@trafford.com
Order online at:
www.trafford.com/robots/04-2160.html

10 9 8 7 6 5 4 3 2

This book is dedicated
in loving memory
to my godson
Matthew Dessmann

PREFACE

$\mathcal{I}$n July of 1989, while attending a church conference in Phoenix, I had the opportunity to have lunch with John Boswell, the Chair of the Department of History at Yale. He was attending the conference to deliver a talk based on a book that he had written.[1] We had a fascinating discussion based on a book he was researching and planned to publish "in about a year or two."(It was published in 1994[2].) Our discussion concerned his trips through Europe and his research efforts in the archives of some of the major European libraries and museums. He informed me that he was searching out original ancient manuscripts regarding religious ceremonies for the blessing of same-sex couples.

I later discussed the luncheon with a close friend, Jim Wulk, who appeared to be as fascinated with the subject as I was. Not long after that discussion, Jim had a relapse of the lymphoma that he thought was cured. He did not survive the relapse. Before he died, he asked me to write an article for a magazine or to write a book regarding gay rights. I told him I would think about it if he would do me a favor. At Jim's funeral, I vowed that somehow, God willing, I would write the book. This is the product of that promise.

The focus of this writing took several avenues over the years. I originally intended to direct the subject matter of this writing toward the Gay Rights Movement. The next avenue focused on supporting a constitutional amendment to be known as "The Non-discrimination Clause". When same-sex marriage became a popular subject of debate, my focus changed to that topic. Finally, I decided to incorporate all three topics into the writing.

I want to publicly thank Bruce Vanis, "Cricket," Rev. Deacon Kevin Smith, and all those who gave me encouragement. I began this book in 1990 and continued for over a decade doing research, writing notes, etc. I also thank all the librarians who put up with me and who helped me over the years.

I need to express my appreciation to Bob for putting up with the stacks of notes, research papers, interviews, books, and other "stuff" that cluttered the dining room. The man has the patience of Job.

I also would like to express my appreciation to Barbara Ardinger who introduced me to Sue Jorgenson; and to Sue, who proofread and edited this writing.

Finally, I need to recognize all those who have helped me recover saved copy when my computer crashed (and that happened frequently).

There are a great number of personal friends who gave me encouragement and support and who have passed away from various illnesses. Among them are Fr. Steve Scherer, Malcolm Loch, Matthew Orley, Fr. Michael Hartyl, Ricky Aulet, Brian Pullock, Del Heider, David Powers, Bob Northrup, Dean James, Pat Lynch, Harry Hughes, Duquense (Duke) Walters, and Bill Hickbar (Olympic Bronze Medal winner).

It is needless to state that getting this writing published produces a great degree of personal satisfaction for me.

---

[1] Boswell, John. **Christianity, Social Tolerance, and Homosexuality.** (Chicago and London: The University of Chicago Press, 1980).

[2] Boswell, John. **Same-Sex Unions In Premodern Europe.** (New York: Villard Books, 1994).

[3] Public Law 104-199, 100 Stat. 2419 (1996).

TABLE OF CONTENTS

INTRODUCTION

$\mathcal{W}$herever it appears in this writing, the term "America" refers to the United States of America to the elimination of all other North and South American countries unless otherwise specified.

It is not intended that this writing be a scholarly dissertation or treatise but, rather, a reasoned presentation.

The debate over homosexual (hereinafter "gay") rights in America, and most specifically the subject of same-sex marriage, is a matter of major social concern, high political profile and national debate. While the gay community is accepted as a minority, as compared to the heterosexual (hereinafter "straight") community, the social, medical/scientific, religious, legal arguments, and claims of the gay community for equal rights appear to bring forth a standard for equal rights that could prevail in a constitutional challenge.

For the purpose of this writing, homosexuals (gays) are persons romantically attracted to other persons of their own gender while heterosexuals (straights) are those romantically attracted to persons of the opposite gender.

The current and specific issue of concern centers on same-sex marriages. It appears that the present political agenda of this country almost dictates a finding and determination by the United States Supreme Court in the near future in favor of current federal law, specifically the Defense of Marriage Act.[3]

This is not a unique situation, given that the efforts of other movements for equal rights have led to the enactment of federal law and constitutional amendments, and are well documented in the literature.

Social tolerance and acceptance of gay lifestyles is well documented throughout ancient and recent history.

Perhaps the foremost authority on this subject is the late John Boswell, a former Professor of History and Chairman of the Department of History at Yale University. Boswell traces social and religious tolerance of gay people from the early Christian era through the late Middle Ages (to the fourteenth century)[4]. Boswell notes that gay people lived harmoniously within Western European society and as part of society without discrimination or persecution. In this regard it was a very homogeneous society. During this period many gay people occupied positions of wealth and power. It was only toward the end of the late Middle Ages when gay people were identified as a sub-culture or minority group and some restrictions and prejudices became noticeable.

One of the greater influences on the change in western social tolerance of gay people was the period following the Great Schism of 1054 between the Orthodox and Roman Christian Churches. Over the following centuries the Roman Catholic Church developed an official intolerance of homosexuality that greatly influenced the social attitudes of members of their Church and, indeed, much of Western society.

The United States has been traditionally perceived as an international advocate for justice and human rights. Under the provisions of its Constitution, all citizens share an undivided right to be equal and are endowed with equal rights, entitlements, and freedoms without discrimination.[5] Since the enactment of that governing instrument, there have been movements by a number of minority groups to obtain equal rights. While these movements differed in approach and method in their quests, they all had in common and purpose the goal of equality. Only a few of these movements or efforts will be referenced here; they are covered extensively in Chapter III.

The first such equal rights movement and its constitutional resolution that has a direct bearing upon this writing is the Dred Scott case of 1846 (Scott v. Sandford).

Two slaves, Dred Scott and his wife, Harriett, sued for their freedom based upon the fact that they had been held in bondage for extended periods in a free territory and then returned to a slave state. The lawsuit between Dred Scott and his owner, Army Surgeon Sandford, was essentially a private lawsuit that became an eleven-year legal struggle culminating in one of the most notorious decisions ever issued by the U.S. Supreme Court. While ruling in favor of Sandford in 1857, the Court failed to consider the larger issues of Negro citizenship and the constitutionality of the Missouri Compromise, which resulted in the Supreme Court holding that Scott had no leave or right to file suit because he was not a citizen of the United States. As a slave, he was considered property. Furthermore, Congress was held to have no power to exclude slavery from the free territories. Therefore, the Missouri Compromise and other legislation limiting slavery were deemed unconstitutional.[7]

As a result, the question of slavery assumed center stage of American debate for many years. In June 1858, Abraham Lincoln, in accepting the Republican nomination for the U.S. Senate from Illinois, uttered the prophetic phrase: "A house divided against itself cannot stand."[8]

On July 14, 1848, a small and obscure weekly newspaper in New York, known as The Seneca County Courier, published a simple notice, consisting of three sentences, inviting women to a discussion of "the social, civil, and religious rights of women." Thus was the Suffragist Movement born. In August 1920, the Nineteenth Amendment to the Constitution became law and women were endowed with full rights of citizenship, including the right to vote.

The third movement was the Civil Rights Movement, which became the political, legal, and social struggle to gain full citizenship rights and equality for black Americans. It expanded to include Americans of Asian and Native American descent. The Civil Rights Movement was first and foremost a challenge to segregation, the system of laws and customs separating blacks and whites, which was used to control blacks after the abolition of slavery in the 1860s. Many believe that the movement began with the Montgomery bus boycott in 1955 and ended with the Voting Rights Act of 1965[9], although there still is debate about when it began and whether it has yet ended.

Finally, in 1967, a constitutional question, which had never been addressed, was argued before and decided by the U.S. Supreme Court.

It had its origins in a June 1958 marriage between two Virginia residents: Mildred Jeter, a black woman, and Richard Loving, a white man. They were married in the District of Columbia pursuant to its laws, and shortly thereafter, they returned to establish their marital abode in Caroline County, Virginia.

During the October Term, 1958, of the Circuit Court of Caroline County, a grand jury issued an indictment charging the Lovings with violating Virginia's ban on interracial marriages (388 U.S. 1, 3). On January 6, 1959, the Lovings pleaded guilty to the charge and were sentenced to one year in jail. The sentence was suspended for 25 years by the trial judge on the condition that the Lovings leave Virginia and not return together for 25 years.

The Lovings appealed and the case was eventually argued before the U.S. Supreme Court on April 10, 1967. On June 12, 1967, the U.S. Supreme Court found that Virginia's statutory scheme to prevent marriages between persons solely on the basis of racial classifications was held to violate the Equal Protection and Due Process Clauses of the Fourteenth Amendment to the Constitution.

These four movements have a direct bearing upon, and are the ancestors of, the Gay Rights Movement. They are discussed extensively in Chapter III, along with the history of the Gay Rights Movement.

The active quest for full and equal rights for gay people began in the 1960s and 1970s. There were several events leading up to the full and organized movement for equal rights.

When World War II ended, the subject of homosexuality was unspoken of in "polite society." The subject was taboo. Most communities denied the existence of homosexuals within their confines, except for one or two "token" gay people whom they could point out to others. Gay people lived among the general population as a sub-culture with a "don't ask, don't tell" mentality (there were a lot of "Uncle Ned bachelors" and "Aunt Alice spinsters").

In 1948, Dr. Alfred C. Kinsey published the result of years of research on sexual behavior[10], with a second report following in 1953[11]. His findings astounded and embarrassed the general public who reacted with shock and outrage, both because Kinsey challenged conventional beliefs about sexuality and because he discussed subjects that were not "socially polite" and proper.

Gay people of this era did not congregate in public. They usually socialized in the privacy of each other's homes. They were a silent and much hidden sub-culture in our society.

Key West, Florida was a popular tourism spot attracting many to the small Key to live and play. During the later part of the 1920s and early 1930s, the Key suffered through a number of calamities causing a tremendous financial erosion of the entire Key. Residents moved out of the Key and real estate values plunged. Many gay persons, who had previously visited and enjoyed the Key, saw a tremendous opportunity and began purchasing real estate and other properties in the Key. Nightclubs, guesthouses, hotels, hostels, and other tourist-friendly establishments opened and prosperity returned to the Key, primarily because of the gay community's investments. Today the area of Key West known as "Old Town" is mainly occupied by gays.

The idea of gays owning public establishments gave rise to a number of "gay-friendly" establishments throughout the United States. Gays began socializing in public, in their own clubs and bars, and the era of exclusive home socializing went into decline. The Key West custom of the Sunday afternoon "Tea Dance" was now common throughout the nation and gay people began to "come out."

With the appearance of gay establishments came a degree of social rejection, outright discrimination, and harassment. People observed entering or leaving these establishments were often publicly "outed." The establishments often became targets for unannounced police raids and other types of public harassment.

There was a two-story structure with a brick and glass storefront, known as the Stonewall Inn, at 57 Christopher Street in Greenwich Village, located in New York's lower Manhattan, which catered to the gay community. This was a gay oriented private club. It became the target of the New York Police Department and harassment raids became common. After two years of unannounced raids, on the last Friday of June 1969, the helmeted Tactical Police Force of the First Division again arrived at the Stonewall Inn. The police entered the club with a warrant alleging the sale of unlicensed liquor. The police ushered the guests out of the club and onto Christopher Street. Soon a crowd of an estimated 500 to 1,000 gathered in front of the club. One burly Stonewall patron threw a metal garbage can, filled with empty liquor bottles, through a police car windshield and, as one news reporter stated, "all hell broke loose." The riot lasted from midnight until two o'clock Saturday morning. There were numerous injuries on both sides and the police made 13 arrests. The event was on the front page of the nation's newspapers that Saturday and Sunday. Gays from surrounding areas began arriving on Christopher Street and a repeat event was experienced on the following Wednesday night. These events are known as the "Stonewall Riots" or simply "Stonewall." This is considered the beginning of the active public movement for gay rights.

The advent of HIV and AIDS during the 1980s sent shock waves through the gay community and the nation. The nation's blood supply was contaminated and efforts toward containing the disease went forward with frantic haste. Death certificates began noting the cause of death from HIV infection. Research efforts developed tests to detect HIV/AIDS and centers were opened across the nation for testing, referral, treatment and public education. The disease appeared to be centered primarily, though not exclusively, in the gay community in America.

Discrimination and harassment toward gays re-appeared in a most hostile and forceful manner and "gay bashing" became familiar. This form of discrimination peaked in the late 1980s and 1990s.

The nation was shocked upon hearing of the death of Matthew Shepard, a 21-year-old gay student at the University of Wyoming who came from the small Wyoming town of Cody. On October 6, 1988, Shepard was brutally murdered and robbed. The motive for the crime was determined to be based upon Shepard's sexual orientation.

On November 30, 1993, three young men went on a spree terrorizing gay men. They abducted Nicolas West from Bergfeld Park in Tyler, Texas, and took him to a gravel pit outside of town, shot him nine times, and left him to die.

On July 4, 2000, the body of 26-year-old Arthur Warren was discovered in Grant Town, West Virginia. Two seventeen-year-old boys, wearing steel-toed boots, kicked Warren (whom they believed was gay) to death in an abandoned house, put his body in the trunk of a dark Camaro, drove him to a gravel strip below the town power plant, placed his corpse on the side of the road, and repeatedly ran over it. The crime was described as a "hate crime."

The body of a man was found murdered at the McFarlin Tennis Courts in San Pedro Park, near San Antonio, Texas. A man was found shot in his car behind the Nacho Baron on San Pedro Avenue and another man was found stabbed to death on East Laurel, near the Pegasus Club. All three of these crimes occurred within one month and within a one-mile radius of San Antonio, Texas' gay club scene.

These are a few examples of the types of extreme hate crimes that targeted gay people. The nation's cry for hate crime legislation was heard from coast to coast and from border to border (including Alaska and Hawaii); it resulted in a majority of states enacting hate crime legislation.

The organized movement to promote gay rights is spearheaded by the Human Rights Campaign and the Gay Rights Movement. The American Civil Liberties Union (ACLU) has undertaken the majority of legal work in promoting gay rights. While much has been accomplished by this effort,[12] little has been accomplished toward the recognition of same-sex marriages and nondiscrimination legislation. Conversely, the effort to ban same-sex marriage has been the successful effort spearheaded by the Family Research Council (in the private sector) and Republican Policy Committee (in the political sector).

It is generally conceded that, if same-sex marriages become legal, some of the gay agenda for equal rights will be accomplished. The effort to legalize same-sex marriages caused fear in the opposition and legislation was introduced to ban same-sex marriages. That legislation passed both houses of Congress and was signed into law on September 21, 1996, as the Defense of Marriage Act.[13] The Act limits marriage to a man and a woman.

With the recently revived movement advocating same-sex marriages, proponents of the Defense of Marriage Act acknowledge that the Act would probably not survive a constitutional test before the U.S. Supreme Court. To this end, the current effort of the conservative political and religious right is to adopt the Act as an Amendment to the United States Constitution. This subject becomes convoluted in recognition that each of the 50 states have the right to establish their own marriage laws and the federal law only comes into play to determine that it is done without discrimination under the Due Process Clause of Section 1 of the Fourteenth Amendment to the Constitution, or if a state can show that such proposed legislation would adversely affect a compelling State interest. A federal law specifically discriminating against a class or group of persons based on sexual orientation could be quite a departure from the mainstream of constitutional law. However, a law that would ban discrimination on the basis of race, color, creed, sexual orientation, national origin/ethnicity, and/or sex/gender would probably complement the provisions of the Fifth and Fourteenth Amendments.

The Universal Fellowship of Metropolitan Community Churches (UFMCC), a gay and gay-friendly Christian denomination, has grown to an international church and supports many efforts of the gay community, including the right to same-sex marriage. The UFMCC has performed numerous same-sex marriages, called "Holy Unions." Although not recognized at civil law, it promotes the concept of equal rights for same-sex marriages. The basis for their decision to perform Holy Unions is centered in the tradition of the early Christian Church.[14]

The question of gay rights, especially the right to same-sex marriage, has appeared on dockets of courts from State Circuit Courts to the Federal Appellate Courts. It is only a matter of time before some of these cases reach the level of the United States Supreme Court.

Our society depends on the court system to resolve a great number of issues. Our courts interpret our Constitution (Federal and state) and our laws and codes as applied against issues coming before them. Based on rules governing evidence and testimony to determine fact and a strict procedure to reach determinations, the jurisprudence system of this country is an excellent example of how an issue of discrimination should be resolved.

On the issue of same-sex marriage, a significant portion of the argument for a constitutional amendment to ban same-sex marriages appeals to emotion rather than to reason. Many of the attitudes opposing gay rights are inherited from generation to generation and, in many cases, are based on misinformation and misguided belief. Placing the issue within a legal court's arena allows the introduction of fact (evidence and testimony) before a fair-minded jury or court to determine a reasoned outcome. Supporting this movement is the basic purpose of this writing.

Primary areas concerning the issue of same-sex marriage (and the Gay Rights Movement) are social tolerance and acceptance, medical and scientific factors, religious beliefs and legal considerations.

"All those whose lives are spent searching for truth are well aware that the glimpses they catch of it are necessarily fleeting, glittering for an instant only to make way for new and still more dazzling insights. The scholar's work, in marked contrast to that of the artist, is inevitably provisional. He knows this and rejoices in it, for the rapid obsolescence of his books is the very proof of the progress of scholarship."[15]

It is assumed that most of the readers of this effort are

peers. You, the readers, are the jury charged with separating fact from fiction, truth from false assumption, and understanding from misconception. Please read with an "open mind" as if you were a juror charged with making a reasoned judgment based solely on the evidence and testimony presented. Feel free to join this debate, but only with researched and proven fact and trusted and tested testimony.

This quest, then, is for truth.

---

[4] Boswell, John. **Christianity, Social Tolerance, and Homosexuality.** (Chicago and London: The University of Chicago Press, 1980).

[5] Articles I through 10, **Constitution of the United States of America.** (In Congress: July 4, 1776.)

[7] MSN. **American Civil War.** (Encarta Encyclopedia, undated document.)

[8] National Center for Public Policy Research. *"A House Divided Against Itself Cannot Stand."* **Historical Documents** (Internet, undated); also adapted from the **Bible**: Luke 11, 17.

[9] Congress determined that the existing anti-discrimination laws were not sufficient to overcome the resistance by state officials to enforcement of the 15th Amendment. The Voting Rights Act was signed into law by President Johnson on August 6, 1965, and was amended in 1970, 1975, and 1982.

[10] Kinsey, Alfred C., W. B. Pomeroy, and C. E. Martin. **Sexual Behavior in the Human Male.** (Philadelphia: W. B. Saunders, 1948.)

[11] Kinsey, Alfred C., W. B. Pomeroy, and C. E. Martin. **Sexual Behavior in the Human Female.** (Philadelphia: W. B. Saunders, 1953).

[12] Most colleges and universities have nondiscrimination policies protecting gay students and employees. Many states, counties, and municipalities also have nondiscrimination policies protecting gay employees and residents' rights. While there is some protection at the federal level, it is not total.

[13] Public Law 104-199, 100 Stat. 2419. (1996).

[14] To be more fully covered in Chapter II.

[15] Pirenne, Henri. Cited in Georges Gerady, **Henri Pirenne, 1862-1935**, Ministere de l'education nationale et de la culture, Administration des services eduatifs. Brussels, 1962.

I

SOCIAL TOLERANCE
—————————— *and* ——————————
ACCEPTANCE

$\mathcal{K}$insey projects that 37% of the American population are homosexual. That figure includes all prisoners. Excluding the prisoners, about 11.3% of the population is gay (9.9% for white, college-educated males and 12.7% for those with less education).[16] Paul Gebhard, Kinsey's successor as director of the Kinsey Institute for Sex Research, spent years reviewing the statistical data from the research. He and other noted scientists found Kinsey to have used extremely stringent research methodology and was very conservative in his findings. A truer and more accurate figure of the number of homosexuals in the population (including the female population) would conservatively approach about 14.7%.[17]

Based on the 2000 census figures, the U.S. Census Bureau

projects a total population of the United States (as of February 29, 2004) at 292,695,290 persons.[18] This projects an estimated population of gay persons at approximately 43,026,208 (excluding prisoners).

Same-sex families are growing and have become a homogeneous part of the social fabric of this nation. The 2000 census shows that same-sex couples (households) live in 99.3 percent of all counties in the United States.[19]

It is accurate to state that gays comprise a significant minority group of the population.

Opponents of the gay rights movement generally feel that homosexuality is a freely chosen life-style and behavior. Such attitudes are heavily influenced by religious teachings and often refer to biblical passages. They believe that gay behavior is intrinsically abnormal, wrong, sinful, unhealthy, and unnatural, and that God created all persons heterosexual. They further hold that sexual orientation is modified by upbringing and environmental factors and not by genetics. This belief also holds that by granting gays equal rights more youth would be encouraged to choose a homosexual life-style.

Those who support the gay rights movement believe that homosexuality is an intrinsic part of one's being and they have attitudes formed or based mostly on scientific studies and findings and on personal awareness. Sexual orientation can have natural variations of heterosexuality and homosexuality that apply to all societies and cultures. They believe that sexual orientation is determined at, or before, birth and is genetically and biologically determined, which eliminates free choice in the matter. Further, they hold that sexual orientation is unchangeable.

Prior to the Kinsey Report the literature is grossly lacking in discussion of or statistics regarding lesbians. This is a very unfortunate finding. It is surmised that most writings were made by men, about men, and for men.

Many "closeted" gay persons experience social, cultural, legal, and psychological or psychiatric problems exceeding that of their straight counterparts. This is especially true of youths between the ages of eleven and twenty. Evidence indicates that gay-oriented males account for more than half of male suicides and suicide attempts.

The American Journal of Health noted:

> "...YRBSS (Youth Risk Behavior Survey
> Surveillance) data from the localities that
> measure sexual orientation show that whatever
> the dimension of sexual orientation measured
> (sexual orientation, identity, sexual behavior,
> or sexual attraction), sexual minority youths
> have higher rates of suicide attempts, victimi-
> zation in school violence, drug and alcohol abuse,
> early onset of sexual behavior, eating disorders
> and teenage pregnancy than other youths. As
> surveys of adolescents in Connecticut, Wisconsin,
> Oregon and Seattle have demonstrated, even a
> measure of sexual orientation as indicted as
> perceived homosexual orientation elicits disturbing
> correlations with deleterious health outcomes."[20]

There is increasing scientific evidence that sexual orientation is determined by biological factors; it is not a matter of choice or the result of environmental, social, or similar non-biological factors. There has been, and continues to be, a substantial amount of research into this subject. However, based on the great body of scientific evidence that already exists, a number of national health oriented organizations have taken a position on the subject.

Some studies have concentrated on monozygotic (identical) twins. These are twins originating from the natural splitting of a single fertilized egg (the zygote). Both halves of the zygote have identical genetic structure. The study focused on identical twins that were separated at birth and who had not been in contact with each other. The consistent conclusion of these studies is that male homosexual orientation is determined at the point of conception of one's genes.

Sexuality researchers hold a common belief that sexual orientation is determined by a pre-existent genetic marker occurring at conception.

In other research, conducted at the Salk Institute by Simon LeVay, a neuroanatomist, the brains of men who died of AIDS were examined. He found that the INAH3 (a hypothalamus structure) differed in size between gay and straight men. This demonstrates that sexual orientation has a biological substrate.[21] It is unknown whether the treatment medication had an effect on the INAH3.

There are existing treatment modalities that attempt to change the orientation of gays known as "reparative" therapy.[22] Some of these modalities use electric shock and other aversion techniques. However, the majority of this type of effort is based on a psychological aversion technique using peer, social, family, and, primarily, religious or spiritual factors in the persuasive technique (a form of "brain-washing"). The majority of this country's reputable health and mental health organizations do not support this type of so-called therapy. The American Psychiatric Association, the American Academy of Pediatrics, the American Medical Association, the American Psychological Association, the American Counseling Association, and the National Association of Social Workers either directly oppose or are highly critical of these types of reparative therapies.[23]

Additionally, the American Psychiatric Association (APA) formulated a Position Statement that reads, in part:

> "Recommendations: 1. APA affirms its 1973 position that homosexuality per se is not a diagnosable mental disorder. Recent publicized efforts to repathologize homo-

sexuality by claiming that it can be cured
are often guided not by rigorous scientific
or psychiatric research, but sometimes by
religious and political forces opposed to
full civil rights for gay men and lesbians.
APA recommends that the APA respond quickly
and appropriately as a scientific organization
when claims that homosexuality is a curable
illness are made by political or religious
groups."[24]

Some of these national health organizations have taken positions supporting some of the rights gays have been seeking. The American Psychiatric Association has adopted the official policy that:

"The American Psychiatric Association supports
initiatives which allow same-sex couples to
adopt and co-parent children and supports all
the associated legal rights, benefits, and
responsibilities which arise from such initiatives."[25]

Additionally, the American Psychiatric Institute adopted the following position:

"The American Psychiatric Association supports
the legal recognition of same sex unions and
their associated rights, benefits and responsibilities."[26]

Opponents to same-sex marriages often contend that marriage is intended for the purpose of procreation. This is a position that simply cannot be defended. To allow that definition of marriage would prevent anyone who is not physically able to, or who prefers not to, have children to be disqualified for marriage, including senior citizens and those with medical conditions resulting from illness or injury, etc.

Beginning with the year 2000, a number of observations concerning the tolerance of gays by our society are noted. There has been a general decline in the incidence rate and severity of hate crimes against gays; twenty-seven states have enacted hate crime legislation, which includes sexual orientation among the criteria;[27] more gays have been "coming out" and are enjoying relatively comfortable social lives; a number of religious denominations now accept same-sex unions and bless them; most major schools of higher learning have, and enforce, non-discrimination policies; major television and cable networks have gay-oriented characters in their story lines[28]; some municipalities have "domestic partner" registers that grant some benefits to gay employees; some municipalities (and some states) ban discrimination in housing and employment; some states allow same-sex couples to adopt minor children. The list goes on.

At one point in our history, virtually every state had sodomy laws. In the 19th century, Pennsylvania became the first state to define sodomy to include oral sex. This definition expanded the sodomy laws to women and made arrests easier. In the mid-1950s, the American Law Institute noted the increasing consensus among legal, criminal, and medical experts that sodomy caused no harm to society. Additionally, the Institute argued that sodomy laws caused harm because it limited freedom in private lives and urged that such laws be overturned. In November 2003 the United States Supreme Court heard a Texas sodomy case and, in a six to three decision, held that the Texas sodomy laws were unconstitutional, and that:

> "The state cannot demean their existence or
> control their destiny by making their private
> sexual conduct a crime.[29]"

By application, sodomy laws in the remaining twelve states

that have them are considered moot.

This is a showing of evidence that the Gay Rights Movement is advancing. However, this is viewed only as a movement toward a goal in the overall quest for total and equal gay rights, which has not yet been achieved.

On February 23, 2004, President George W. Bush announced that he was in favor of a constitutional amendment that would ban same-sex marriages. On February 24, 2004, the CNN cable network station posed as their "Question of the Day": "Should the U.S. Constitution be amended to ban same-sex marriages?" By late morning (11:35 a.m. CST) over 394,192 votes were counted —one of the largest responses to the "Question of the Day" feature. 42% or 167,097 voted YES, while 58% or 227,095 voted NO.[30] While not considered a scientifically accurate poll, it is reflective of the general attitude toward the question.

As used herein, the term "social tolerance" refers to the public acceptance of personal variation or peculiarity in matters of opinion, life-style, personality, or belief. "Social tolerance" is distinguished from "approval". A people may well tolerate a life-style or belief without approving of it.

At this point, in American society, it appears that the general population tolerates (although some do not approve of) the gay sub-culture.

The high political and social profile of the issue of same-sex marriage occupies a significant amount of coverage by the media and in the U.S. Congress. The issue seems to concentrate on the emotional appeal of the term "sanctity of marriage."

The words "marriage," "wedding," and "civil union"[31] are common terms often used in the same-sex marriage debate. The words appear to carry varying definitions and meanings to different people. Of specific note is the word "marriage." The term "sanctity of marriage" seems to connote a religious or spiritually elevated status of marriage beyond the words "wedding" and "civil union."

Webster gives a number of definitions for marriage. Some of the definitions include reference to a union between a man and a woman. However, one of the definitions is "any close or intimate union."[32] Webster defines wedding as "the act or ceremony of becoming married" and "the marriage ceremony with its attendant festivities.[33] Civil union is not found listed in Webster. Common usage of this phrase appears to show that a civil union can be between any two consenting adults who obtain a proper and legal certificate or license, and, once the ceremony is performed, all the attendant rights, privileges, benefits, responsibilities, and duties in marriage are conferred upon the couple as a result of the civil union.

For the purposes of this writing, the definition of marriage and civil union will be considered identical. The term wedding will refer to the ceremonial aspects of becoming married.

It is interesting to note that a greater number of people prefer the term civil union for same-sex marriage. For some reason the term marriage connotes something beyond the conferring of legal rights.

Some of the proponents for a ban on same-sex marriage contend that, historically, no society has ever tolerated same-sex marriages prior to recent times.[34] Contrary to that position or observation are historical facts documented in the literature.

The "Gilgamesh Epic" is an early Middle Eastern literary work, written in cuneiform on twelve clay tablets about 4,700 years ago.[35] It depicts a Babylonian king who ruled the city of Uruk (formerly called Erech in the Bible, now known as Al Warka, Iraq). It also depicts the relationship between King Gilgamesh and Enkidu. The two formed an intimate relationship and lived together until the death of Enkidu. King Gilgamesh followed the general Hammurabi Code (a system of laws governing relationships between kingdoms and the territories in between, but not within the kingdom itself). Gilgamesh, as king, held the sole power of determining who could and who could not live together in intimate relationships (marriages) in

Uruk. As such, his relationship with Enkidu was the same as any other marriage.

In 1964, Egyptian archaeologist Mounir Basta discovered a number of images of two men in intimate poses (caressing, holding hands, and kissing) on the walls of an ancient tomb dating to the Fifth Dynasty. The tomb was constructed for two men to cohabit, Niankhkhnum and Khnumhotep, both of whom held identical titles in the palace of King Niuserre as the "Overseer of the Manicurists in the Palace of the King."[36]

Edward Gibbon noted that "of the first fifteen emperors Claudius was the only one whose taste in love was entirely correct," meaning heterosexual.[37] W. C. Firebaugh added, "But Claudius was a moron."[38] Homosexuality among the Romans was wholly integrated within their society but in quite a dispassionate manner. Roman law did not classify homosexual acts as illegal but did have laws against forcible rape, including homosexual rape. At its prime, the Roman Empire influenced most of Western Europe.

The noted historian, John Boswell, traces numerous similar accounts of same-sex unions throughout ancient history and into the late Middle Ages.[39] Certainly, the early Christian Church recognized and blessed same-sex unions.[40]

Same-sex couples living in committed relationships for ten, twenty, thirty, and more years find themselves denied many rights and privileges married couples enjoy.

A significant number of gay closeted men who, for fear of persecution and discrimination factors, and who yield to family and societal pressure, enter into opposite gender marriages. In many, if not most, of these marriages children are produced. It is only later in life, if at all, that these gay men come out of the closet and usually go through divorce. This is an alarming realization that affects a great number of people in our society. The ramifications in these situations can be extensive and convoluted.

Before the Defense of Marriage Act[41] was signed into law

on September 21, 1996, Henry J. Hyde, Chairman of the Judiciary Committee of the House of Representatives, wrote the General Accounting Office requesting, within his letter of September 5, 1996, that the General Accounting Office "identify federal laws in which benefits, rights, and privileges are contingent on marital status."

Barry R. Bedrick, the Associate General Counsel for the United States General Accounting Office, responded to Chairman Hyde's request in a four page letter with extensive enclosures. He identified thirteen general categories in federal laws (U.S. Codes) where benefits, rights, and privileges are contingent upon marital status. Those categories are:

1. Social Security and related programs, Housing, and Food Stamps
2. Veteran's Benefits
3. Taxation
4. Federal Civilian and Military Service Benefits
5. Employment Benefits and related laws
6. Immigration, Naturalization, and Aliens
7. Indians
8. Trade, Commerce, and Intellectual Property
9. Financial Disclosure and Conflict of Interest
10. Crimes and Family Violence
11. Loans, Guarantees, and Payments in Agriculture
12. Federal Natural Resources and related laws
13. Miscellaneous Laws

[Note: The first five categories are considered the most pervasive.]

Outside of these federal entitlement categories, there are many other federal and non-federal rights, privileges, and benefits that are contingent upon marital status that negatively affect same-sex couples. Some of them are identified as: adoption rights (including adoption rights of one partner of a same-sex couple where the other partner is a natural parent); state and local tax laws; hospital visitation rights when a same-sex partner becomes seriously ill; health insurance coverage for a non-employed same-sex partner; employment; housing; surviving spouse status in probate matters including property inheritance; protection in worker's compensation cases and unemployment; parenting rights, separation and divorce; and many others. The rights, entitlements and privileges contained in these classifications exceed a thousand ways in which same-sex couples are discriminated against.

Included in, and in addition to the thirteen federal categories previously set forth, the following is a partial list of rights, entitlements, and privileges inherent in marriage:

- Autopsy examination consent
- Burial rights of service member's dependents
- Child custody in divorce proceedings
- Cohabitation on military and other federally controlled properties
- Community property control, division, acquisition, and disposition
- Exemption from conveyance tax
- Court notice of probate proceedings
- Death benefit for surviving spouse for government employees
- Domestic violence protection orders
- Existing homestead lease continuation of rights
- Regulation of condominium sales to owner-occupants exemption
- Funeral and bereavement leave
- Joint adoption and foster care
- Joint tax filing
- Property tax exemption for homes of totally disabled veterans
- Income tax deductions, credits, rates exemption, and

estimates

- Insurance licenses, coverage, eligibility, and benefits organization of mutual benefits societies
- Legal status with stepchildren
- Making, revoking, and objecting to post-mortem anatomical gifts
- Making spousal medical decisions
- Spousal non-resident tuition deferential waiver
- Payment of wages and worker's compensation benefits after death of worker
- Permission to make arrangements for burial or cremation
- Right of survivorship of custodial trust
- Right to change surname upon marriage
- Right to enter into pre-nuptial agreement
- Right to inheritance of property
- Right to sue for tort and wrongful death
- Right to child support after divorce
- Spousal privilege and confidential marriage communications
- Spousal immigration benefits
- Spouse of veteran medical care discount
- Status as next-of-kin
- Visitation privileges to imprisoned spouse
- Visitation privileges to spouse in hospital

One could argue that, if civil unions were legal, the exact same benefits, privileges, rights, and entitlements would be conferred that are inherent in marriage. However, the reality is that, in those government entities where civil unions are recognized, only limited benefits, privileges, rights, and entitlements are granted and such civil union is not universally recognized in other jurisdictions. There is no question that overt discrimination now exists in the United States and has been formalized and condoned under the Defense Of Marriage Act.

President Clinton signed Executive Order 13087 in 1998 prohibiting discrimination in the federal civilian workforce. President Bush allowed it to stand. However, there is no prohibition against discrimination in employment based on sexual orientation for all other employees. In 38 states gays can be fired, barred from renting an apartment, or barred from restaurants, hotels, and other public accommodations because of their sexual orientation. Employment is just one area of discrimination experienced by gays. If one party to a same sex relationship becomes seriously ill, the other party can be barred from hospital visitation and from making health care decisions (in the absence of a durable power of attorney for health care).

Our probate laws bar the survivor of a same-sex relationship from inheritance tax advantages or from surviving property rights to which a surviving spouse would be entitled.

The Family and Medical Leave Act of 1993 allows employees to take up to twelve weeks' leave from employment for a seriously ill spouse, child, parent, or parent-in-law. That same right does not apply to same-sex couples.

The foregoing are only a few examples of over a thousand ways against which same-sex oriented persons are routinely discriminated.

Our society's attention is now becoming focused on the question of gay rights and, in particular, same-sex marriage. People are now in the sometimes uncomfortable position of consciously re-considering their personal positions and attitudes regarding the same.

The most gay-friendly twelve states in the United States are identified as: the District of Columbia, Vermont, California, Connecticut, New Jersey, Minnesota, Rhode Island, Massachusetts, New York, New Hampshire, Oregon, and Washington.

Other countries have faced and resolved the question we face today. Same-sex marriages or civil unions are allowed in a number of countries. Among these are Belgium (since 2003),

Denmark (since 1989), Finland (since 2002), France (since 1999), Germany (since 2001), the Netherlands (since 2001), Norway (since 1993), Portugal (same as common-law marriages), South Africa (working to be the same as common-law marriages), and Sweden (since 1995). There is legislation pending in the countries of Britain (to give legal recognition), Canada (the provinces of Ottawa and British Columbia have same-sex marriage entitlement laws) and Switzerland (Zurich and Geneva have recognized such laws since 2003).

Challenges to the laws banning same-sex marriages in several states (Hawaii, California, and Massachusetts) reached the various states' Supreme Courts and were determined to be unconstitutional. Literally hundreds of marriage license were issued to same-sex couples while the state legislatures rushed to begin the process to amend the state constitutions to ban same-sex marriages, usually by adopting language similar to that in the Defense of Marriage Act.

There are three psychological mind-sets, or perceptions, that developed in the Western society through the last half of the eighteenth, nineteenth, and twentieth centuries. It is difficult for our modern culture to realize, perceive, or understand ancient societies' perception of romantic love.

The first such perception is that, in our modern culture, romantic love is the primary interest of society as reflected in an overwhelming proportion of popular music, art, and literature. It appears that modern culture's central focus is "...on the seeking out, celebration of, or lament over romantic love..."[42] We tend to assume, based upon our cultural conditioning, that the same was the focus of pre-modern cultures and societies.

> "In other cultures and pre-modern Western
> societies other subjects have formed the
> primary material of public culture: celebration
> of heroic figures or events; reflections on
> the seasons, observations on the success,

failure or precariousness of agricultural
cycles; histories of families (in which
romantic love plays a small role, if any);
explorations and elaborations of religious
or political traditions."[43]

A second mind-set is that of an expectation of romantic love
and marriage. This is a unique perception as it was almost absent in most other societies. Most people in other societies did
not marry for love but for profoundly different reasons. Many
men, in pre-modern society, had multiple wives —sometimes
hundreds. The relationships between the single man and over
one hundred wives could hardly be called a romantic commitment. In pre-modern Europe marriage was basically a property
arrangement at the beginning, followed by the rearing of children and finally love. Few, if any, married for love but many
did find love over the length of their relationship.

The third mind-set, as evidenced in the nineteenth and
twentieth centuries, is the attitude toward the subject of same-
sex relations. Except for the past few decades, such a subject
was not mentioned in "polite" company —it was taboo, a re-
vulsion. Sometimes it was referred to as "the unmentionable
vice" or "the sin that cannot be named" or "the love that dare
not speak its name."

Other countries also accepted same-sex unions and relationships. Examples of this would be Chinese men and women
under the Yuan and Ming dynasties,[44] Japanese warriors in early modern times,[45] Native Americans of various tribes (mostly
before they were dominated),[46] various African tribes well into
modern times,[47] male and female peoples of the Middle East,[48]
South-East Asia,[49] Russia,[50] other parts of Asia,[51] and South
America.[52] Boswell does an excellent presentation of same-sex
unions and relationships in Western Europe from the early
Christian era through the 14th century.[53]

During this early period in history a man was allowed sexual relations with anyone within his power including house-

hold maids, concubines, and others. Generally, only the wife could be property-vested to receive from her husband. Men were allowed as many wives as they could afford. According to the Bible, Solomon, the wisest of the patriarchs, had seven hundred wives and three hundred concubines.[54] However, the most common type of heterosexual marriage in all Mediterranean societies (the legally required form in Athens and Rome) was monogamous —one male and one female.

A highly significant aspect of Roman law was the overall tendency of European and Mediterranean society to emphasize consent and marital affection as the primary determinants of valid marriage, a view based on Roman law: "It was not cohabitation, but consent that makes marriage."[55] In Roman-ruled Egypt, marriage contracts often specified that the husband may not have concubines of either gender in the house.

By far the most common type of same-sex relationships in both pre-modern Europe and in the modern West was that two women or two men in a love relationship had no legal standing for property or status.

Harmodius and Aristogiton were a pair of male lovers who founded Athenian democracy by violence and war at Pelopidas and Epaminondas, to Alexander and Bagoas. Plato noted that:

> "Our own tyrants learned this lesson
> through bitter experience, when the love
> between Aristogiton and Harmodius grew so
> strong that it shattered their power.
> Wherever, therefore, it has been established
> that it is shameful to be involved in sexual
> relationships with men, this is due to evil
> on the part of the legislators, to despotism
> on the part of rulers, and to cowardice on the
> part of the governed."[56]

Gorgidas created an army of three hundred men, composed of pairs of male lovers known as the "Sacred Band of Thebes." As Plutarch later explained, "even Plato calls the lover a friend 'inspired of God.'"[57]

There are numerous examples of successful same-sex couples with life styles similar to heterosexual couples.

During this era, and through the early Christian era, there were, generally, three well-known types of same-sex formal unions that are described in some detail by Boswell[58] and paraphrased here.

1.Strabo, a noted ethnographer living during the beginning of the Christian era, gives a description of an abduction ritual required to establish a legal relationship between male lovers in Crete.

"They (the Cretans) have peculiar laws
regarding love. For they acquire their
lovers not by persuasion but by abduction.
The lover advises friends three or more days
before hand that the abduction is going to
take place. If they sequester the youth or
he avoids the designated road it would be a
considerable disgrace, as if they acknowledged
that he was unworthy of such a lover. When
they encounter each other, if the abductor
is the young man's equal or superior in social
class and other respects, they pursue and
restrain him only a little, in observance of
the law, and then willingly relinquish him.
If [the abductor] seems unworthy, they take the
youth away.
The pursuit is not over until the youth is
finally brought to the abductor's quarters. They
regard as the most worthy of love young men who

are outstanding not in beauty, but in character
and attractiveness. After giving the youth a
present, he takes him to the country, to any spot
he wishes. The witnesses to the abduction accompany
them, and after feasting and hunting for a couple of
months (for it is not permitted to keep the young
man away longer than this), they return to the city.
The young man returns bearing as gifts a
military outfit and an ox and a chalice (these
are specified by law) and other things besides,
so many that the friends must contribute to cover
the expenses. He sacrifices the ox to Zeus and
gives a feast for those who accompanied them, at
which he states publicly in regard to his relationship with his lover whether he is pleased about
it or not. The law prescribes this so that if
any force was used for the abduction he can at
this point seek redress and extricate himself
[from the relationship].
It is a disgrace for young men who are
good-looking and from good families not to
have lovers, as if this were the consequence
of their own conduct. Those who have been
abducted are called 'partners' and enjoy special privileges:
at dances and races they are given
places of honor, and they are allowed to wear
finer clothes than others —what their lovers
gave them. Not only that, but even when they
are older they wear distinctive clothing, which
indicates that they are special. For they call
the beloved 'special,' and the lover his 'friend.'
These are their legal arrangements regarding love."[59]

This abduction requirement for same-sex union in Crete
includes all of the elements of the European marriage tradition:

witnesses, gifts, religious sacrifice, a public banquet, a chalice, a ritual change of clothing for one partner, a change of status for both, a public statement at the banquet (consent) and a honeymoon.

Zeus was considered the ruler of the gods and he maintained a permanent relationship with a beautiful Trojan prince, Ganymede, after abducting him and carrying him off to heaven. They were the most famous same-sex couple of the ancient world.

2.There is a description of a life-long relationship between two males who lived on the north shore of the Black Sea (the Crimea).

"We consider appropriate to what you do
in regard to marriage for a long time and doing
everything similar so that we might not fail to
obtain the friend, or be rejected. And when a
friend has been preferred to all others, there
are contracts for this and the most solemn oath,
both to live together and to die, if necessary,
for each other, which we do. From the point at
which we have both cut our fingers and let the
blood run into a chalice, dipped the tips of
our swords in it, and both drunk from it together,
there is nothing that could dissolve what is
between us.
It is allowed to enter into such contracts
at most three times, since a man who had many
such relations would seem to us like a
promiscuous and adulterous woman, and we would
not consider that his devotion was as strong if
it was divided among many affections."[60]

3.The third type of formal same-sex union was the legal

practice of adoption, known as "collateral adoption." One man adopted another man as his brother either de facto or in some official way.

Adoption was an extremely common practice among the Romans. It was a method of providing heirs outside of parenthood or just to bequeath wealth, position or status to a loved one. In the majority of cases, men (including bachelors) adopted younger persons as sons or daughters by the *adrogatio* or *adoption* method. For the adoptee the advantages are obvious, but the disadvantage was in being subjected to the authority of the adoptive person, which could be awkward and confining.

Under the early Roman Empire, men began adopting brothers, rather than sons who would become heirs, without becoming children by way of adoption. This could be legally accomplished simply by declaring the same in the presence of witnesses. The newly adopted "brother" thus acquired a claim on the adopter's property and estate to a degree greater than a natural brother. The advantage to this arrangement was that the adopted brother did not come under the control of the adopter and probably did not change his name or status. As Boswell states: "Given that 'adopt a brother' was a specific imperial expression for establishing a relationship with a homosexual lover, and that contemporaries understood Roman heterosexual marriage to be a kind of collateral adoption, with the wife becoming, in essence, a sister, it seems clear enough that such adoptions were understood as a means of establishing in law a same-sex union."[61]

In summation, the three forms of same-sex marriages in these ancient times were abduction, blood-mingling, and brotherly adoption.

It is necessary to understand that the attitude toward homosexuality and same-sex unions in America, prior to the last half of the eighteenth, nineteenth, and twentieth centuries was more open and accepting than during the last half of the 1700s, the 1800s and most of the 1900s, and that the concept of marriage was not based on romantic love but on arrangements of mutual convenience (sometimes necessity). Same-sex relationships and same-sex unions were common and unremarkable, though not legally recognized.

The attitude of Americans, prior to the 1700s, was quite open, tolerating and accepting of same-sex couples. Since the 1700s, that attitude grew to be unaccepting and intolerant. During the second half of the twentieth century society began showing tolerance and some acceptance. At the turn of the millennium, a new awareness, openness, and general tolerance of gay life style(s) became evident. This relatively new trend toward acceptance is clearly a major factor leading to the current national debate over same-sex marriage.

Recent media headlines indicate an increasing trend in spiritual awareness, noting that the Lutherans, Presbyterians, and Reform Jews have ended restrictions on gays; some now sanction same-sex unions.

Increasingly, the attitude of "live and let live" and "I'm OK, You're OK" is noted, especially among the younger generation.

It is difficult for many in this country (and other countries, as well) to comprehend that the United States, which is universally recognized as the defender and advocate for justice and human rights, could have such a discriminatory law as the Defense of Marriage Act on its books. There is a growing realization in the minds and hearts of a majority of Americans that this injustice must be faced and completely resolved in the near future.It would truly be unfortunate if the pending political debate to ban same-sex marriage becomes an appeal to emotions rather than to rationality.

It is considered probable that the current Defense Of Marriage Act will not survive a constitutional challenge. The international community perceives the United States as a protector, defender and advocate for freedom, equality and human rights. In recognition of the disenfranchisement of over 40 million Americans, it is held that the United States Constitution should be amended to include a nondiscrimination clause to ban discrimination on the basis of race, color, creed, sexual orientation, national origin/ethnicity and/or sex/gender.

---

[16] Kinsey, Alfred C., W. B. Pomeroy, and C. E. Martin. **Sexual Behavior in the Human Male.** (Philadelphia: W. B. Saunders, 1948).

[17] Kinsey, Alfred C, W. B. Pomeroy, and C. E. Martin. **Sexual Behavior in the Human Male.** (Philadelphia: W. B. Saunders, 1948), and **Sexual Behavior in the Human Female.** (Philadelphia: W. B. Saunders, 1953).

[18] U. S. Census Bureau of the Economics and Statistics Administration of the United States Department of Commerce: *Census Report Year 2000.*

[19] Ibid. 16.

[20] Sell, R. L. and J. B. Becker. **Sexual Orientation Data and Progress toward Healthy People 2010.** *American Journal of Health* 91 CW.

[21] LeVay, Simon. The Sexual Brain. (MIT Press, 1994).

[22] A position that homosexuality is a developmental disorder and can be reversed through reparative therapy is held by the National Association for Research and Therapy of Homosexuals.

[23] American Counseling Association Passes Resolution to Oppose Reparative Therapy. NARTH Web site

[24] The American Psychiatric Association, Position Statement, *Therapies Focused on Attempts to Change Sexual Orientation (Reparative or Conversion Therapies),* 2002. APA Web site.

[25] Ibid. . (Adoption and Co-parenting of Children by Same-sex Couples: Position Statement)

[26] Ibid. (Same Sex Unions: Position Statement)

[27] Human Rights Campaign Foundation, **The State Of The Family,** *Laws and Legislation Affecting Gay Lesbian, Bisexual and Transgender Families.* (Washington, D.C., 2002.).

[28] For example, Showtime's **Queer as Folk** and **The L Word,** NBC's **Will and Grace,** etc.

[29] **Lawrence and Garner v. Texas,** Docket No. 02-0102 (U.S. Supreme Court).

[30] CNN, **Home Page,** *Question of the Day* (Internet, www.CNN.com, 02/20/2004).

[31] The term "Domestic Partnership" is not used here as the meaning reflects a relationship other than marriage or civil union.

[32] Webster. **Webster's New World Dictionary of the American Language**, College Edition. (Cleveland and New York: The World Publishing Company, 1958).

[33] Ibid.

[34] Stanton, Glenn T. *Is Marriage in Jeopardy*, in **CitizenLink**, 'Focus on Social Issues.' (Internet, 08/27/2003).

[35] See Appendix I for a more complete description.

[36] From the Internet.

[37] Gibbon, Edward, **History of the Decline and Fall of the Roman Empire.** (1789 edition)

[38] Firebaugh, W. C.. **The Satyricon of Petronius Arbiter.** (New York, 1966).

[39] Boswell, John. **Same-Sex Unions in Premodern Europe.** (New York: Villard Books, 1994).

[40] Ibid.

[41] Public Law 104-199, 100 Stat. 2419. (1996)

[42] Boswell, John. **Same-Sex Unions in Premodern Europe.** (New York: Villard Books, 1994).

[43] Ibid.

[44] Hinsch, Bret. **Passions of the Cut Sleeve.** (Berkley: 1990).

[45] Schalow, Paul. **The Great Mirror of Male Love.** (Stanford: 1990).

[46] Williams, Walter, **The Spirit and the Flesh:** *Sexual Diversity in American Indian Culture.* (Boston: 1997).

[47] Evans-Pritchard, Edward. **The Azande: History and Political Institutions.** (Oxford: 1971).

[48] Dickson, Harold. **The Arab of the Desert: A Glimpse into Badawin Life in Kuwait and Saudi Arabia.** (London: 1951).

[49] Layard, John W. **Stone Men of Malekula.** (London: 1942).

[50] Luzbetak, Louis. **Marriage and the Family in Caucasia: A Contribution to the Study of North Causasian Ethnology and Customary Law.**

(Vienna: 1951).

[51] Jochelson, Waldemar. **The Koryak.** (Leiden: 1905-08).

[52] Gandavo, Pero de Magalhaes de. **Historia da Provincia Santa Cruz.** (Sao Paulo: 1964).

[53] Boswell, John. **Same-Sex Unions in Premodern Europe.** (New York: Villard Books, 1994).

[54] The Bible. 1 Kings 11:3, The wives were of royal blood, the concubines not.

[55] Nuptias non concubitus, sed consensus facit (50.17.30).

[56] Symposium 182; cf. Plutarch Moralia 767.

[57] Symposium 179A.

[58] Boswell, John. **Same-Sex Unions in Premodern Europe.** (New York: Villard, 1994).

[59] Strabo. **Geography.** 10.4.21

[60] Boswell, John. **Same Sex Unions in Premodern Europe.** (New York: Villard Books, 1994).

[61] Ibid.

II

SPIRITUAL TOLERANCE
and
RELIGIOUS ACCEPTANCE

Because of the diverse conditions of humans, it happens that some acts are virtuous to some people, as appropriate and suitable to them, while the same acts are immoral for others, as inappropriate to them.

—Saint Thomas Aquinas [Summa theologiae]

*I*nvariably, the term "sanctity of marriage" keeps arising in debates over same-sex marriage. This veiled inference that somehow there is a spiritual protection inherent in marriage is most reflective of a Judeo-Christian origin.

Marriage is a legal and binding contract("the contract of marriage") between two legal adults who have obtained a marriage license, freely entered into, witnessed with consideration being exchanged (rings and vows) and presided over by a person legally vested by the state. The spiritual aspect arises when the marriage is performed by a clergyperson[62] and the ceremony is often referred to as "being wed in the eyes of God."

As indicated previously, society places married persons in a unique status. Marriage is, essentially, between two people who expect a permanent and exclusive partnership, which creates a value upon the union conferring special rights, privileges, entitlements, and responsibilities not otherwise available to unmarried persons. The key word is "expectation." If a marriage left the status of a couple unchanged it would not be perceived as a marriage by most of society, and it would thus be rendered valueless.

Some jurisdictions recognize a common law marriage. This is when a couple live together, as a married couple, for a specified number of years without the benefit of a marriage license or wedding ceremony. Where, and when, such a common law marriage is recognized, the full marriage entitlement to rights, privileges and responsibilities is conferred. The legislation regarding common law marriages is left to the individual states.

The purpose of marriage in our modern society is centered upon romantic monogamous love.

Historically, it is necessary to comprehend the attitude toward love, matrimony and sex in the Greco-Roman culture in pre-modern times:

> "This is what it means to be married: to
> have sons one can introduce to the family and
> neighbors, and to have daughters of one's own
> to give to husbands. For we have courtesans for
> pleasure, concubines to attend to our daily
> bodily needs, and wives to bear children
> legitimately and to be faithful wards of our homes."[63]

The Bible is considered to be many things, among which is that it is a written historical record reflecting many ancient customs and traditions. Much of the Old Testament of the Christian Bible was passed down by strict oral tradition from one generation to another until finally the accounts were put into writing. These earliest writings, or scrolls, became the sacred Torah of Judaism. The marriage tradition/custom is referred to throughout the Old and New Testament. For instance, in one of the earliest of biblical passages, the story of Noah and the Ark,[64] Noah takes his wife, his sons Shem, Ham and Japheth, and his sons' wives aboard the Ark. God directs Noah to build an Ark and to:

> "…go on board the ark, yourself, your sons,
> your wife, and your sons' wives along with you."[65]

Family units, including that of husband and wife existed from the earliest of biblical times.

Little is said of the specific marriage ceremony except that it was a common custom to exchange something as a symbolic gesture indicating the marriage pronouncement. In the Book of Ruth we find the marriage of Ruth to Boaz pronounced when Boaz and town elders, as witnesses, were standing near the town gate and:

> "…Now in former times it was the custom
> in Israel, in matters of redemption or exchange,
> to confirm the transaction by one of the parties
> removing his sandal and giving it to the other.
> In Israel this was the form of ratification
> in the presence of witnesses. So when the man
> with right of redemption said to Boaz, 'Purchase
> it for yourself', he took off his sandal.
> Then Boaz said to the elders and all the
> people, 'You are witnesses this day that I buy
> from Naomi all that belonged to Elimelech, to
> Chilion and to Mahlon. You are my witnesses too

that I buy Ruth the Moabitess, Mahlon's widow,
to be my wife, to keep the name of the dead man
in his inheritance, so that the dead man's name
may not die out among his brothers and at the gate
of his town.'"[66]

The value of Ruth, in this transaction, was that of property. There was no romantic relationship, only the need to produce heirs and to carry on the family name.

We also know that marriages were celebrated with family, relatives and friends. Consider the wedding feast at Cana in the New Testament, to which Jesus and his disciples had been invited.[67] Marriage customs varied throughout the world with the single, common idea that some act was taken to symbolize a commitment.

Boswell traces the evolution of marriage from about 100 A.D. to about 1000 A.D. in, predominantly, Western Europe. It was shortly thereafter that the Americas were discovered and the missionaries and other religious came to these shores with their beliefs, customs and practices. About 284 years later, the United States of America was founded as a nation.

We have, in so many ways, adopted the religious or spiritual attitudes, beliefs and positions that we inherited from birth and that had been passed from one generation to the next. It appears that only time, serious debate, and/or a realignment of values can produce a shift or change in such deeply-ingrained attitudes and beliefs.

Opponents of same-sex marriage often come from a predetermined, fixed mind-set that views homosexuality in a negative context. This is often the product of misinformation and/ or inherited attitudes. In this regard, the religious right often attempts to validate their position by claiming biblical origins for their attitudes and opinions. There are seven specific scripture passages that are usually cited in the condemnation of homosexuality: Deuteronomy 23:17-18, Genesis 19:4-11, Leviticus 18:22, 20:13-14, 1 Corinthians 6: 9, 1 Timothy 1:10, and Romans 1:26-27. Many of the political and Christian far-right evangelists ("fundamentalists") often make use of these citations and quote them as "one-liners". This type of substantiation is often referred to as "bible-bingo" in certain circles. However, each of these passages should be reviewed in the total context of their intent, and when, why, and by whom they were written.[68] Below are the referenced passages. .

Deuteronomy 23:17-18
"He shall live with you, among you,
wherever he pleases in any of your towns he
chooses; you are not to molest him.
There must be no sacred prostitute among
the daughters of Israel, and no sacred prostitute
among the sons of Israel. You must not bring
to the house of Yahweh your God the wages of
a prostitute or the earnings of a dog whatever
vow you may have made, for both are detestable
to Yahweh your God."

The fundamentalists would have us believe that the reference to sacred prostitution among the Israelite sons and daughters is a condemnation of homosexuality.

In reality, this refers to two specific historical occurrences —one is fertility cult worship and the other relates to the temple cult worship of the idol or god, Baal.

The worship of the fertility god, usually in temples dedicated to the god Baal, was a very common practice in ancient cultures. Some young girls would present themselves at the temple, and some young men would castrate themselves (to become eunuchs) and present themselves at the temples to become male and female prostitutes. It was part of the cult practice for members to make an annual retreat to the temple and have sexual relations with one of the temple prostitutes (it didn't matter

if it was same or opposite-sex). Recall the story of the young
Hebrews Daniel and his companions (Hananiah, Mishael and
Azariah) at the Court of King Nebuchadnezzar.[69] The chief
eunuch renamed them. Daniel was named Belteshazzar, Hananiah bcame Shadrach, Mishael became Meshach, and Azariah
became Abednego. Nebuchadnezzar tried to persuade Daniel,
Shadrach, Meshach and Abednego to follow the cult worship.
The young Israelites refused to defile themselves while in the
pagan temple, which was dedicated to the god Baal.

These are the same cult practices that so many of the
prophets were preaching against in keeping the First Com-
mandment: "I am the Lord your God. Thou shall not have
strange gods before me."

Genesis 19: 4-11 ("The Sin of Sodom")
"They had not gone to bed when the house
was surrounded by the men of the town, the men
of Sodom both young and old, all the people
without exception. Calling to Lot they said,
'Where are the men who came to you tonight?
Send them out to us so that we may abuse them.
Lot came out to them at the door, and having
closed the door behind him said, 'I beg you,
my brothers, do no such wicked thing. Listen,
I have two daughters who are virgins. I am
ready to send them out to you, to treat as it
pleases you. But as for the men, do nothing to
them, for they have come under the shadow of my
roof.' But thcy replied, 'Out of the way! Here
is one who came as a foreigner, and would set
himself up as a judge. Now we will treat you
worse than them.' Then they forced Lot back
and moved forward to break down the door. But
the men reached out, pulled Lot back into the
house, and shut the door. And they struck the

men who were at the door of the house with blindness, from the youngest to the oldest, and they never found the doorway."

[NOTE: In this version, the translators use the term: "...so we may *abuse* them." Other translations use the term: "...so we may *know* them."]

Previous to this passage, Abraham learns that God intends to destroy Sodom and pleads with him not to destroy the town if but ten good men could be found in the town. Two angels of God, disguised as two traveling men, met Lot at the town gate and Lot convinced them to spend the night at his house. Lot made them a meal and it was about bedtime when the men of Sodom arrived at Lot's front door. Following this passage, the angels advise Lot to take his two daughters and "run for the hills." God destroyed Sodom and Gomorrah with fire and brimstone.

The fundamentalists would have us believe that the "Sin of Sodom" referred to the sexual threats of the men of Sodom with the implication that they all were homosexuals and that was the sin. This is far from the truth. If all of the men of Sodom were homosexuals the town of Sodom could not continue. The vast majority of the men appear to be heterosexual men attempting to use sex to dominate and humiliate the new arrivals to the community. The proposition in Genesis is, obviously, to forcefully gang rape the two travelers. Few, if any, cultures throughout history tolerated forced rape, much less gang rape. Also operating in this passage is the intolerable sin of inhospitality. In the days of the Old Testament it was a sacred duty and obligation to meet the needs of travelers passing by one's home or entering a city. Jesus underscored the sin of inhospitality in Sodom, as found in Luke 10:10-20:

"But whenever you enter a town and they do

not make you welcome, go out into its streets
and say, 'We wipe off the very dust of your town
that clings to our feet, and leave it with you.
Yet be sure of this: the kingdom of God is very
near.' I tell you, on that day it will not go as
hard with Sodom as with that town."

There are several beautiful biblical same-sex love stories. Consider the Book Of Ruth in the Old Testament. After Naomi's husband (Elimelech) died, her two sons (Mahlon and Chilion) married Moabite women. Mahlon and Chilion were both killed in battle leaving Naomi and her two daughters in law. Orpah was with child and returned to her own family while Ruth stayed on with Naomi. Over the years, a strong emotional bond grew between the two. Naomi became concerned for Ruth because as Naomi grew older she was worried that Ruth would have nobody to care for her in her old age. She could not convince Ruth to return to her family. Finally, Naomi decided to leave the Moab country and return to her own country (where she held considerable real estate) to force Ruth to return to her own people. When Naomi told Ruth of her plans, Ruth pleaded: "Do not press me to leave you and to turn back from our company, for

'wherever you go, I will go,
wherever you live, I will live.
Your people shall be my people,
and your God, my God.
Wherever you die, I will die
and there I will be buried.
May Yahweh do this thing to me,[70]
and more also,
if even death should come between us!'"[71]

Naomi relented and Ruth accompanied her back to her

homeland. Once there, Naomi contrived to have Ruth marry Boaz (see earlier references to the purchase of Naomi's lands and Ruth). In this manner, Naomi was assured of Ruth's future. Ruth had a child, Obed, and Naomi became his nursemaid. Obed became the father of Jesse and Jesse became the father of King David.

Another beautiful and romantic scripture story concerns King David (when he was in his teen years) and Jonathan (the son of King Saul). After David slew Goliath, he was summoned by Saul:

"After David had finished talking to Saul,
Jonathan's soul became closely bound to David's
and Jonathan came to love him as his own soul.
Saul kept him by him from that day forward and
would not let him go back to his father's house.
Jonathan made a pact with David to love him as
his own soul; he took off the cloak he was wearing
and gave it to David, and his armour too, even
his sword, his bow and his belt."[72]

And again:

"Once again Jonathan swore the solemn oath
to David because he loved him as his own soul."[73]

Jonathan and David made a pact to meet privately in the fields. David would hide and Jonathan would bring his servant to retrieve his arrows.

"Jonathan gave his weapons to his
servant and said, 'Go and carry them to the
town.' When the servant went off, David
rose from beside the hillock and fell with
his face to the ground and bowed down three

times. Then they kissed each other and both
shed many tears. Then Jonathan said to David,
'Go in peace.' And as regards the oath that
both of us have sworn in the name of Yahweh,
may Yahweh be witness between you and me,
between your descendants and mine for ever."[74]

Following Jonathan's death, David publicly lamented,

"O Jonathan, in your death I am stricken,
I am desolate for you, Jonathan my brother.
Very dear to me you were, your love to me
more wonderful than the love of a woman."[75]

Please note that David did not say "like a brother" or "more than a brother," but "my brother"[76] although the two were not related.

Unlike other ancient cultures, the literature of the Jews has little reference to same-sex couplings. In ancient Israel three factors combined which made for a negative attitude toward homosexual relations.

First, there was a great emphasis on procreation. The need to have children was a guarantee of being taken care of in later years. Israel was a relatively small nation surrounded by larger and more powerful nations. Israel needed warriors to protect themselves —just to hold their own. Moreover, their God (Yahweh) had told them that one of their chief responsibilities was to be fruitful and multiply. Their religion centered upon being God's people, and one was a member of God's people by being born into it. The covenant with God and its blessings were passed down through family lines. Their belief was not of a personal immortality; rather, the future of being God's people would be maintained through descendants. It was considered a terrible curse to be sterile and have no children. If a man died without leaving any sons to carry on his name, there were special laws that required his brother or another close male relative to have sexual intercourse with the decedent's wife to sire a son for him. Homosexuality was contrary to the concept of the necessity to have children.

Second, Israel's aversion to same-sex relations among men related to their relatively small and weak nation. Defeat in battle was somewhat commonplace for Israel's relatively small army. It was common practice in the ancient world to humiliate one's conquered enemy. The form of humiliation was often anal intercourse or rape. To rape another man was a symbol of domination (being treated like a woman), causing destruction to his dignity and masculine honor; it was humiliating and emasculating. The Egyptians frequently practiced anal rape on their conquered victims.

An example of male humiliation is recorded in 2 Samuel 10.[77] King David sent some of his male servants to Hanun, King of the Ammonites on a mission of kindness and good will. Hanun was convinced that the servants were only there to study the town to make an invasion easier. Hanun humiliated David's servants by shaving off half of each man's beard and cutting their clothes halfway up to the buttocks. The male egos of these Israelites were shattered; they were completely devastated and greatly shamed.

The third factor contributing to Israel's intolerance of homosexual relations among men was Israel's concern in isolating itself from the cultic practices of their neighbors who worshiped the fertility gods that practiced cultic prostitution. The sexual rites of the fertility cults were considered acts of worship, a ritual of offering believed to be pleasing to the deities.[78]

Despite Israel's negative attitude toward homosexual relations, the Hebrew Scripture does recite several same-sex, loving relationships, which probably included sexual relations.

Present day fundamentalists often cite from the Old Testament. These isolated quotes were usuallly not interpreted as comments on homosexual behavior or practices by classical Jewish scholars and authorities. In medieval Europe, the many references to the 'sin of Sodom' were not interpreted as homosexual conduct but of the extreme breach of hospitality. As Boswell notes:

> "The medieval rabbinical authority
> Nachmanides composed a long commentary on
> Genesis 19, which is almost identical to
> the opinion of most twentieth century com-
> mentators, arguing that the sin of the
> Sodomites was clearly and unequivocally a
> sin against hospitality, not sexual purity."[79]

Two strong convictions of the ancient Middle East were the absolute dignity of men and the absolute sacredness of the guest. Both convictions are violated here. That is the "Sin of Sodom."

Leviticus

[18:22] "You must not lie with a man as with a woman. This is a hateful thing."

[20:13-14] "The man who lies with a man in the same way as with a woman: they have done a hateful thing together; they must die, their blood shall be on their own heads."

The fundamentalists usually claim this directly addresses the homosexual question.

These two passages occur in the "Holiness Code." This was directed and addressed to the Hebrew people who were surrounded by pagan and polytheistic peoples. This code of laws was to keep them set apart visibly as a reminder to them to maintain their religious purity and as a witness to others. It was mandated to keep them separate and to maintain their cultic purity. In context it is quickly apparent that these verses occur within passages that refer to the god Molech, who was a fertility god. They are couched among prohibitions of a list of practices common to fertility worship —incest, bestiality and adultery. It is apparent that these passages are specifically directed at the abuses of fertility cult worship. The fertility god Molech was often found in temples dedicated to the god Baal.

I Corinthians 6:9
"You know perfectly well that people
who do wrong will not inherit the kingdom
of God; people of immoral lives, idolaters,
adulterers, catamites, sodomites…"

I Timothy 1:10
"…for those who are immoral with
women or with boys or with men, for liars
and for perjurers —and for everything else
that is contrary to the sound teaching. ."

Romans 1:26-27
"That is why God has abandoned them
to degrading passions: why their women have
turned from natural intercourse to be consumed
with passion for each other, men doing
shameless things with men and getting an
appropriate reward for their perversion."

Extreme-right evangelists often cite these passages from the New Testament to prove condemnation of homosexuals. However, this again refers to temple and cult practices. The term "Sodomite" in 1 Corinthians references the mandate of hospitality. The referenced portions from 1 Timothy and 1 Romans are obviously directed toward the issues of the fertility cult and pagan temple worship.

From the beginning there have been problems with the translation and interpretation of scripture. Of interest here is that in Latin, Greek, Aramaic and other ancient languages there was no term or word for homosexual. The word most often used was a variation of the term sodomite. That variation does not appear in the Old or New Testament.

Boswell, after meticulously investigating the earliest known scrolls of most of these scriptures and tracing the translations through the centuries, has published his conclusions and opinions. Other scriptural scholars, historians, and authorities are in general agreement with Boswell on this finding:

> "The New Testament takes no demonstrable
> position on homosexuality. To suggest that
> Paul's references to excesses of sexual
> indulgence involving same-sex eroticism is as
> unfounded as arguing that his condemnation of
> drunkenness implies opposition to the drinking
> of wine. At the very most, the effect of
> Christian Scripture on attitudes toward homo-
> sexuality could be described as moot. The most
> judicious historical perspective might be that
> it had no effect at all. The source of antigay
> feelings among Christians must be sought
> elsewhere."[80]

Early Christian tradition appears to take the same position as Boswell.

> "For is there anything better than a
> wife who is chaste, domestic, a good house-
> keeper, a rearer of children; one to gladden
> you in health, to tend you in sickness, to be
> your partner in good fortune, to console you
> in misfortune; to restrain the mad passion of

youth and to temper the unseasonable harshness
of old age? And is it not a delight to acknowledge
a child who shows the endowments of both parents?"[81]

It is important to understand the role of women during
biblical times. Women are not often referenced in ancient writings. Their role was secondary to men. Men wrote about men,
for men. However, we do know that, during these times, it
was thought that only men could create new life through their
seed. Women were nothing more than incubators that carried a
child to birth. Married couples always needed children to care
for them in their old age. There was no other type of retirement
—children inherited and took care of their parents. This was
primarily a male role. Women were considered near property
as their true value was only as an incubator for children and
maintaining the day-to-day status of the household. Men were
allowed multiple wives but women were only allowed one husband.

It is truly unfortunate that Boswell was not able to continue his studies and publish his historical findings from 1500
A.D. to the present. However, the basis of knowledge we have
from his writings do project that spiritual attitudes change and
evolve over time.

The subject of numerous ancient cults (fertility, harvest,
etc.) and gods (Molech, Baal, etc.) was previously covered.
However the Christian, Judaic, and Muslim (Islam) God has
not been specifically covered. In the cited religions, the monolithic God of Abraham is the God that is worshiped and all
trace their spiritual lineage to that God (Yahweh, Allah).

At about the beginning of the fourteenth century, Western
Europe developed a most fervent negative attitude against homosexuality and considered it the worst sin.[82] The reason for
this transition of attitude has never been adequately explained.
Dante (1265-1321), while making a most detailed ranking of
punishments of his time, ranked sodomites on the highest pla-

teau of eschatological punishments of his time, placing it just outside the gates of heaven on the top rung of purgatory (along with an excess of heterosexual passion). This placement was the highest or closest to heaven as compared to all other sinners in purgatory. The Greek-speaking Christian world's attitude change was not as critical, but was existent.

In these areas, where negative attitudes developed toward homosexuality, same-sex unions were viewed as legitimizing "the sin that could not be named." Eventually, homosexuality and same-sex unions were forbidden by law and considered to be outside the church. Boswell notes that versions of ceremonies for same-sex blessings and unions virtually disappeared from most of Western Europe and noted that no Latin versions of the ceremonies survived. He further notes that even the Greek versions are scarce.[83]

In Eastern Europe, ceremonies of same-sex unions continued and were performed between Christian and non-Christians. Of note is that many of these were Muslims since the Ottomans had an increasing presence in this area. The Christian hierarchy took a dim view of these "mixed marriages."

Boswell notes that ceremonies for same-sex unions were performed in Albania into the early twentieth century.[84]

Nuptial Offices first appeared about the seventh century and developed into Formal Nuptial Offices by the time of the first millennia. Prior to that an ecclesiastical ceremony was considered an honor reserved for the wealthy, powerful, elite, and to those lucky enough to secure one. The early Christian Church did routinely bless opposite-sex and same-sex unions. Boswell scoured Europe in search of these ancient canons and photographed the same in the archives of some of Europe's main libraries.[85] In reviewing some of these liturgies, the names of highly acclaimed paired male saints appear, including (as noted earlier) Saints Serge and Bacchus, well known archetypes of Christian same-sex couples.

In the United States about 78.3% of the population identify with one of the cited religions (76.5% Christian, 1.3% Jewish, 0.5% Islamic). 13.2% are nonreligious or secular.[86]

All three religious groups have many similar beliefs and many opposing views. One area of consistent similarity is the concept of who God is. There is agreement that God is the Supreme Being over all of creation.

Individuals who identify with these three religions find difficulty in specifically defining their God. Individual definitions differ from each other and often from the official view of their religions. In this regard, the theological identification of God is basic to each of these religions and is similar.

Those who condemn homosexuality on religious grounds often do so without a full understanding or appreciation of what and/or who homosexuals are, or without understanding the spiritual position to which their particular religious denomination adheres in relating to creation and what may be the true accurate theological view of that denomination.

However, it is not necessary to give a complete theological explanation of who God is. It may be perceived to be an oversimplification but, basically, God is good. God is 100% good and can do no evil. God can only create that which is good. God creates humans, and humans are good.

"God created man in the image of himself, in
the image of God he created him, male and female
he created them."[87]

"God saw all he had made, and indeed it was
very good. Evening came and morning came:
the sixth day."[88]

This is the point many are confused about. As previously outlined, science has determined that sexual orientation is determined at, or prior to, birth —at a point where genes are created. Therefore, God has created a person's sexual orientation

—it is God gifted and, whatever it is, it is good. It is as simple as that! God expects that the gifts he gives us be used for good. However, God also gives us free will and choice in using his gifts to us. Loving and caring relationships between people are good. This is where the good versus evil debate falters regarding the subject of homosexuality. Sexual orientation is what a person is. What a person does with that gift is who that person is. This truism applies to all people.

In the Roman Catholic and Orthodox Christian religions same-sex unions were accepted until the Middle Ages. Of note (among others) is the relationship between Saint Serge and Saint Bacchus, whose union was blessed and who died together as martyrs.[89]

Slavery is an evil that is obvious to most of our society today. Yet it was only about 150 years ago that slavery was abolished following the bloodiest war this nation ever experienced. It was only about 84 years ago, following the Suffragist Movement, that women were granted their full constitutional rights and the Fourteenth Amendment to the Constitution was enacted. It was only 40 years ago when the Voting Rights Act was signed and segregation ended (if it truly has). It was only 37 years ago when the Supreme Court held that to prevent marriages between persons solely on the basis of racial classifications was a violation of the Equal Protection and Due Process Clauses of the Fourteenth Amendment. These enumerated movements were all based on how God created different peoples, and all were successful. In 1969 the Gay Rights Movement began. It still exists (as does the bias, bigotry, discrimination, and denial of rights) and, by the grace of God, will hopefully realize success in the near future.

At a time when the people of the original Thirteen Colonies felt oppressed and discriminated against, our Forefathers drafted a Declaration of Independence that reads, in part:

"We hold these truths to be self-evident, that

all men are created equal, that they are endowed
by their Creator with certain unalienable Rights,
that among these are Life, Liberty and the pursuit
of Happiness."[90]

During very recent times religious attitudes have begun to
change. The news media has carried reports of Christian denominations, as well as non-Christian religions, endorsing and
blessing same-sex unions and lifting restrictions on gays. This
includes Lutheran (under headline: "Lutherans uphold same-
sex unions"),[91] Judaism (under headline: "Reform rabbis sanction gay unions"),[92] and Presbyterian (under headline: "Presbyterians vote to end restrictions on gays")[93]. There appears
to be a spiritual movement based on enlightened attitudes to
tolerate, if not to accept, gays.

The international community perceives the United States
as a protector, defender and advocate for freedom, equality and
human rights. In recognition of the disenfranchisement of over
40 million Americans, it is held that the United States Constitution be amended to include a nondiscrimination clause to
ban discrimination of the basis of race, color, creed, sexual orientation, national origin/ethnicity and/or sex/gender.

---

[62]In the majority of states, marriages can be performed by a Judge, designated Court Commissioner, Notary Public (in some jurisdictions), and
by members of the clergy. Clergy refers to an ordained person of a religious organization that holds tax-exempt status as a "religious organization" with the U. S. Internal Revenue Service.

[63] Demosthenes, **Against Neara** 122, quoted by Anthenaeus, 13.573b., as
quoted and cited in Boswell's **Same-Sex Unions in Premodern Europe**.

[64] Jones, Alexander, Ed. **The Jerusalem Bible**. Garden City, New York:
Doubleday & Company 1966.

Genesis. 6:10.

[NOTE: **The Jerusalem Bible** was selected for all Scripture references because it is considered one of the foremost scholarly written versions of the Bible. Under the direction of Alexander Jones, 27 of the world's most respected and renowned Scripture scholars collaborated on this translation. Fundamentalists rely virtually solely upon the King James Version of the Bible.]

[65] Ibid Genesis 6:18..

[66] Ibid Ruth 4, 7-10.

[67] Ibid . John 2:1-12.

[68] Ibid. . See NOTE following.

[69] Ibid Daniel. (The entire book).

[70] "May Yahweh do this thing to me" suggests a physical sign similar to cutting her throat.

[71] Ibid. 1:16-18. [NOTE: This passage is often referred to as the first marriage vow.]

[72] Ibid . 1 Samuel 18:1-5.

[73] Ibid . 1 Samuel 20:17.

[74] Ibid . 1 Samuel 20: 40-43.

[75] Ibid. . 2 Samuel 1:26.

[76] As in the Epic of Gilgamesh, the term "my brother" connotes a fraternal bond beyond that of an actual brother or that of a close friend. The reference is romantic, fraternal and conjugal.

[77] Ibid. 2 Samuel 10:1-6.

[78] Pulling, Rev. Jeffrey. **Homosexuality In The Cultural Setting of Ancient Israel**. (New York: Samaritan College, 1986).

[79] Boswell, John. **Same-Sex Unions in Premodern Europe.** (New York: Villard Books, 1994).

[80] Boswell, John. **Christianity, Social Tolerance, and Homosexuality.** (Chicago and London: The University of Chicago Press, 1980).

[81] Dio, Cassius, 56.3.3-4 (LCL, Dio's Roman History 7, trans. Earnest Cary London: 1924.

[82] Boswell, John. **Christianity, Social Tolerance, and Homosexuality.** (Chicago and London: The University of Chicago Press, 1980). See Chapter 10 therein for discussion and documentation.

[83] Boswell, John. **Same-Sex Unions in Premodern Europe.** (New York:

Villard Books, 1994).

[84] Ibid.

[85] Examples of some of these unions are set forth in Appendix II.

[86] Kosmin, Barry A. and Seymour P. Lachman. **American Religious Identity Survey.** (New York: Graduate School of the City University of New York, 2001).

[87] Genesis 1:27

[88] Ibid. Genesis 1:31

[89] Boswell, John. **Same-Sex Unions in Premodern Europe.** (New York: Villard Books, 1994). [**The Passion of SS. Serge and Bacchus**]

[90] In Congress. The Declaration of Independence of the Thirteen Colonies. (Washington, D.C.: National Archives. 1776).

[91] Milwaukee Journal Sentinel, June 2, 2001 edition.

[92] Milwaukee Journal Sentinel, March 30, 2000 edition.

[93] Milwaukee Journal Sentinel, June 17, 2001 edition.

III

PUBLIC TOLERANCE
and
LEGAL ACCEPTANCE

*T*he Gay Rights Movement has existed in this country for decades. Total and equal rights for all gays are the quest of the movement. Some gains have been realized but the goal has not been achieved. There is increasing social tolerance and acceptance of gays by the general society but the protection of rights is not guaranteed, and there is significant opposition being expressed by the political and religious right toward gays gaining these rights.

There have been other national movements toward the quest for freedom and equal rights.

In 1846 a slave named Dred Scott and his wife, Harriet, sued for their freedom in a St. Louis city court. The odds were in their favor. They had lived with their owner, an Army surgeon named Sanford, at Fort Snelling, then in the free Territory of Wisconsin. The Scotts' freedom could be established on the grounds that they had been held in bondage for extended periods in a free territory and were then returned to a slave state. Courts had ruled this way in the past. However, what appeared to be a straightforward lawsuit between two private parties became an eleven-year legal struggle that culminated in one of the most notorious decisions ever issued by the United States Supreme Court.

On its way to the Supreme Court, the Dred Scott case grew in scope and significance, as slavery became the single most explosive issue in American politics. By the time the case reached the high court, it had come to have enormous political implications for the entire nation. Before the Court read the decision, President-elect James Buchanan quietly learned of the decision and used the decision to support the Supreme Court in his inaugural address on March 4, 1857.

On March 6, 1857, in the courtroom located in the basement of the U. S. Capitol, the feeble, nearly 80-year-old Chief Justice Roger B. Taney read the two hour-long opinion of the court.[94] The opinion was that slaves were not citizens of the United States and, therefore, could not expect any protection from the Federal Government or the courts. It continued to state that Congress had no authority to ban slavery from a Federal territory; it effectively nullified part of the Missouri Compromise (territory acquired from France in the Louisiana Purchase of 1803). This opinion moved the nation a step closer to civil war.

The decision in *Scott v. Stanford*, considered by legal scholars to be the worst ever rendered by the Supreme Court, was overturned by the Thirteenth and Fourteenth Amendments to the Constitution which abolished slavery and declared all persons born in the United States to be citizens of the United States.

The Civil War ended the quest for slaves to become freemen and, with the 1865 surrender of General Lee of the Confederacy to General Grant of the Union at Appomattox Court House, the slavery question was ended in the United States. The Thirteenth Amendment to the Constitution was ratified on December 6, 1865, and provides:

"Section 1. Neither slavery nor involuntary
servitude, except as a punishment for crime
whereof the party shall have been duly convicted,
shall exist within the United States or any place subject
to their jurisdiction."

"Section 2. Congress shall have power to enforce
this article by appropriate legislation."

Women's rights became the quest of the Suffragist Movement, which began with an obscure newspaper announcement on July 14, 1848. Women did not have the equal rights of men, including the right to vote. The Suffragist Movement began somewhat slowly but grew throughout the country and ended with the ratification of the Nineteenth Amendment to the Constitution on August 18, 1920. The Nineteenth Amendment provides:

"The right of citizens of the United States
to vote shall not be denied or abridged by
the United States or by a State on account
of sex."

"Congress shall have power to enforce this
article by appropriate legislation."

The Civil Rights Movement began with the Montgomery bus boycott[95] in 1955. It was first and foremost a challenge to segregation (the system of laws and customs separating blacks and whites)[96] that was used to control blacks after slavery was abolished in the 1860s.

The Civil Rights Movement recognized that the protections afforded in the Thirteenth, Fourteenth, and Nineteenth Amendments to the Constitution were not sufficient to guarantee the rights of blacks in many areas, especially their voting rights.

Segregation was often called "the Jim Crow System" named after a character in a minstrel show from the 1830s who was an old, crippled black slave embodying negative stereotypes of blacks. Segregation was widespread in the Southern states following the end of Reconstruction in 1877. Politicians passed local and state laws that specified certain places "For Whites Only" and others for "Colored." Blacks had separate schools, transportation, restaurants, and parks —usually poorly funded and inferior to those of whites.

There were concerted efforts to disenfranchise the blacks in many areas. The Civil Rights Movement was partially directed at breaking the grip of state disenfranchisement but achieved only modest success. The murder of voting-rights activists in Philadelphia and Mississippi gained national attention. Finally, the unprovoked attack on March 7, 1965, by state troopers on peaceful marchers crossing the Edmund Pettus Bridge in Selma, Alabama, en route to the state capitol in Montgomery, persuaded President Johnson and Congress to overcome Southern legislators' resistance to effective voting rights legislation. President Johnson issued a call for a strong voting rights law and hearings began soon thereafter on the bill that would become the Voting Rights Act of 1965. On August 6, 1965, the Act was signed into law by President Johnson, temporarily suspending literacy tests, and providing for the appointment of federal examiners (with the power to register qualified citizens to vote), in those jurisdictions that were covered according to a formula provided in the statute. In addition, under Section 5 of the Act, covered jurisdictions were required to obtain preclearance for new voting practices and procedures from either the District Court for the District of Columbia or the United States Attorney General. Section 2 of the Act closely followed the language of the Fifteenth Amendment, and applied a nationwide prohibition of denial or abridgment of the right to vote on account of race or color.

The Voting Rights Act did not include a provision prohibiting poll taxes, but directed the Attorney General to challenge its use. In Harper v. Virginia State Board of Elections,[97] the Supreme Court held Virginia's poll tax to be unconstitutional under the Fourteenth Amendment. Between 1965 and 1969 the Supreme Court also issued several key decisions upholding the constitutionality of Section 5 and affirming the broad range of voting practices for which preclearance was required. The Supreme Court found, in part, in a 1966 decision[98] upholding the constitutionality of the Act that:

> "Congress had found that case-by-case
> litigation was inadequate to combat wide-spread
> and persistent discrimination in voting,
> because of the inordinate amount of time
> and energy required to overcome the obstructionist
> tactics invariable encountered in these lawsuits.
> After enduring nearly a century of systematic
> resistance to the Fifteenth Amendment, Congress
> might well decide to shift the 'advantage of
> time and inertia from the perpetrators of the
> evil to its victims.'"

During Congressional hearings, extensive testimony was taken regarding the ways in which voting electorates were manipulated through gerrymandering, annexations, adoption of at-large elections and other structural changes to prevent newly-registered black voters from effectively using the ballot. Additional testimony showed voting discrimination that had been suffered by Hispanic, Asian and Native American citizens. Amendments to the Voting Rights Act of 1965 were made in 1970 and 1975. The 1970 Amendment extended Section 5 of the Act for five years and the 1975 Amendment extended Section 5 of the Act for an additional seven years and provided protections from voting discrimination for minority-language citizens. This action validated the Supreme Court's broad interpretation of the scope of Section 5 preclearance.

In 1973, the Supreme Court held certain legislative multi-member districts to be unconstitutional under the Fourteenth Amendment on the ground that they systematically diluted the voting strength of minority citizens in Bexar County, Texas. This decision in White v. Regester[99] strongly shaped litigation through the 1970s against at-large systems and gerrymandered redistricting plans. However, in Mobile v. Bolden[100] the Supreme Court required that any constitutional claim of minority vote dilution must include proof of a racially discriminatory purpose, a requirement that was widely seen as making such claims far more difficult to prove.

In 1982, Congress determined that Section 5 of the Act should be renewed for an additional twenty-five years. Congress also adopted a new standard, which went into effect in 1985, providing how jurisdictions could terminate (or "bail out" from) coverage under the special provisions of Section 4. Additionally, after extensive hearings, Congress decided that Section 2 should be amended to prohibit vote dilution, according to essentially the same objective factors employed in White v. Regester,[101] but without a requirement of proof of discriminatory purpose.

Mildred Jeter, a Negro woman, and Richard Loving, a white man, were both residents of Virginia who married in the District of Columbia.

They returned to Virginia and established their home in Caroline County. At the October Term, 1958, of the Circuit Court [388 U.S. 1, 3] of Caroline County, a grand jury issued an indictment charging the Lovings with violating Virginia's ban on interracial marriages. On January 6, 1959, the Lovings pleaded guilty to the charge and were sentenced to one year in jail. The judge offered to suspend the sentence on the condition that the Lovings leave the state of Virginia and not return to Virginia together for 25 years.

The Lovings appealed the decision and the case was eventually argued before the United States Supreme Court on April 10, 1967. Chief Justice Warren delivered the Court's decision on June 12, 1967, finding that Virginia's statutory scheme to prevent marriages between persons solely on the basis of racial classifications was held to violate the Equal Protection and Due Process Clauses of the Fourteenth Amendment.

Another interesting discrimination case was heard by the Supreme Court involving a gay Eagle Scout leader whose position as assistant scout master of a New Jersey troop was revoked when the Boy Scouts learned that he was an avowed homosexual and gay rights activist.

James Dale filed suit in the New Jersey Superior Court, alleging, *inter alia,*[102] that the Boy Scouts had violated the state statute prohibiting discrimination on the basis of sexual orientation in places of public accommodation. The Superior Court's Chancery Division granted summary judgment for the Boy Scouts, but its Appellate Division reversed in pertinent part and remanded. The State Supreme Court affirmed the holding, *inter alia,* that the Boy Scouts violated the State's public accommodations law by revoking Dale's membership based on his avowed homosexuality. Among other rulings, the court held that application of that law did not violate the Boy Scouts' First Amendment right of expressive association because Dale's inclusion would not significantly affect members' ability to carry out their purposes; determined that New Jersey has a compelling interest in eliminating the destructive consequences of discrimination from society; that its public accommodations law abridges no more speech than is necessary to accomplish its purpose; and distinguished Hurley v. Irish-American Gay, Lesbian and Bisexual Group of Boston, Inc., 515 U.S. 557, on the ground that Dale's reinstatement did not compel the Boy Scouts to express any message.

The Boy Scouts appealed to the U.S. Supreme Court and the matter was argued April 26, 2000.[103] The Court held in part:[104]

> "Applying New Jersey's public
> accommodations law to require the Boy Scouts
> to admit Dale violates the Boy Scouts' First
> Amendment right of expressive association.
> Government actions that unconstitutionally
> burden that right may take many forms, one
> of which is intrusion into a group's internal
> affairs by forcing it to accept a member it
> does not desire. *Roberts v. United States Jaycees,*
> 468 U.S. 609, 623. Such forced membership is
> unconstitutional if the persons presence
> affects in a significant way the group's
> ability to advocate public or private viewpoints.
> *New York State Club Assn., Inc. v. City of New
> York,* 487 U.S. 1, 13. However, the freedom of
> expressive association is not absolute; it can
> be overridden by regulations adopted to serve
> compelling state interests, unrelated to the
> suppression of ideas that cannot be achieved
> through means significantly less restrictive
> of associational freedoms (*Roberts, 468 U.S.,
> at 623*). To determine whether a group is
> protected, this Court must determine whether
> the group engages in "expressive association."
> The record clearly reveals that the Boy Scouts
> does so when its adult leaders inculcate its
> youth members with its value system. See *id.,*[105]

at 636. Thus the Court must determine whether
the forced inclusion of Dale would significantly affect the Boy Scouts' ability to
advocate public or private viewpoints. The
Boy Scouts asserts that homosexual conduct is
inconsistent with the values embodied in the
Scout Oath and Law, particularly those
represented by the terms 'morally straight' and
'clean,' and that the organization does not
want to promote homosexual conduct as a
legitimate form of behavior. The Court
gives deference to the Boy Scouts' assertions
regarding the nature of its expression, see,
*Democratic Party of the United States v.
Wisconsin ex rel.*[106] *LaFollette,* 450 U.S. 107,
123-124."

The discussion continues outlining that Dale, who is one
of a group of gay Scouts who have become community leaders
and are open and honest about their sexual orientation, would
interfere with the Scout's choice not to propound a point of view
contrary to its beliefs. The Court found for the Boy Scouts and
160 N.J. 562, 734 A. 2nd 1196, was reversed and remanded. It
held that the right of the Scouts trumped Dale's right.

There are numerous other movements and law cases concerning bias, bigotry and discrimination that could be outlined
here. However, it appears that the foregoing adequately out-
lines the legal history of the important case findings that relate
to this writing.

Interestingly, there is a case law addressing the engagement
in intimate sex acts by consenting adults in the privacy of their
own homes. The change in sodomy laws over the past few decades is an example of a more enlightened judiciary.

In 1982, Michael Hardwick was a bartender in a gay club
in Atlanta. When his shift was over he left the bar drinking

a beer and threw the container in a trash can. Atlanta police cited him for public drinking. There was some confusion over the appearance date on the ticket (it said "Wednesday" but gave Tuesday's date). Hardwick failed to appear in court and a bench warrant for his arrest was issued. Although he paid the court fine for the offense, the warrant was not retracted. A police officer took the extraordinary step of going to his home at 3:00 a.m. to serve the warrant. A roommate answered the door and indicated Hardwick's room. The officer entered a bedroom and saw Hardwick engaged in sodomy (oral sex) with a male partner and arrested him. Fulton County's district attorney decided not to prosecute the case (a felony that carried a prison sentence of up to 20 years). Hardwick hired the Atlanta law firm of Meadows, Ichter & Trigg to represent him. Attorney Bowers of that firm decided to challenge the law on the basis that it violated Hardwick's privacy rights. The 11th Circuit Court of Appeals agreed, but Michael Bowers, Georgia's Attorney General, appealed to the U. S. Supreme Court.

The Bowers v. Hardwick[107] case was heard by the United States Supreme Court, and the decision handed down upheld the constitutionality of Georgia's sodomy law that criminalized oral and anal sex in private between consenting adults. By a 5-4 vote, the Supreme Court held, in part:

"The Georgia statute is constitutional.

(a) The Constitution does not confer a
fundamental right upon homosexuals to
engage in sodomy. None of the fundamental
rights announced in this Court's prior
cases involving family relationships,
marriage, or procreation bear any resemblance
to the right asserted in this case. And
any claim that those cases stand for the
proposition that any kind of private sexual

conduct between consenting adults is
constitutionally insulated from state
proscription is unsupportable.

(b) Against a background in which many
States have criminalized sodomy and still
do, to claim that right to engage in
such conduct is 'deeply rooted in this
Nation's history and tradition' or 'implicit
in the concept of ordered liberty' is,
at best, facetious.

(c) There should be great resistance to expand
the reach of the Due Process Clauses to cover new
fundamental rights. Otherwise, the judiciary
necessarily would take upon itself further
authority to govern the country without
constitutional authority. The claimed right
in this case falls far short of overcoming this
resistance.

(d) The fact that homosexual conduct occurs
in the privacy of the home does not affect
the result. *Stanley v. Georgia,* 394 U.S. 557,
distinguished.

(e) Sodomy laws should not be invalidated
on the asserted basis that majority belief
that sodomy is immoral is an inadequate rationale
to support the laws."

The decision to uphold sodomy laws became the law of the
land for about 17 years. Michael Hardwick died in Gainesville,
Florida on June 13, 1991 from complications of HIV infection.
His obituary did not disclose either his sexual orientation or his

role in challenging the Georgia sodomy law.

In 1960 every state had a sodomy law. By 2003, only 13 states had a sodomy law. Four of them (Kansas, Oklahoma, Missouri and Texas) prohibit oral and anal sex between same-sex couples. The other nine (Alabama, Florida, Idaho, Louisiana, Mississippi, North Carolina, South Carolina, Utah and Virginia) ban consensual sodomy for everyone.

On September 17, 1998, John G. Lawrence, a fifty-nine year old man, was in his Houston apartment with a guest, thirty-five year old Tyron Garner. A neighbor, Roger Nance, 41, phoned police and reported a man behaving erratically with a gun. Deputy Joseph Quinn arrived at an apartment building east of Houston about 10:30 p.m. and met Nance who directed him to apartment 833, Lawrence's apartment. The deputy entered through the unlocked door with his weapon drawn. After finding no one with a gun, Deputy Quinn (later wrote in his report that he) "observed [Lawrence] engaged in deviate sexual conduct, namely, anal sex, with another man." The other man was Tyron Garner, 31. Both Lawrence and Garner were handcuffed and arrested.[108] Lawrence and Garner spent the night in jail and were released the following morning on bail. Eventually, they were each fined two hundred dollars for violating Texas Penal Code, Section 21.01 (Texas' Sodomy Law).

Lawrence and Garner appealed to a district appeals court and the three-judge panel reversed their conviction. The full nine-judge appeals court reversed the reversal. The Texas Court of Criminal Appeals (Court of Appeals of Texas, Fourteenth District)[109] refused to reverse the lower court. The matter was then appealed to the United States Supreme Court. The United States Supreme Court accepted the case and it was argued on March 26, 2003 and decided on June 26, 2003. The decision of the Court of Appeals of Texas, Fourteenth District, was reversed and remanded. The previously cited Bowers case from Georgia came into direct play in reaching the decision. The specific finding was:

"*Held:* The Texas statute making it a crime
for two persons of the same sex to engage in
certain intimate sexual conduct violates the
Due Process Clause."

Justice Kennedy delivered the opinion of the Court. The
opinion and the rationale for it are quite lengthy with numerous case citations. However, it mst be realized that these findings constitute a sound basis for arguing against the Defense of
Marriage Act and provides an avenue to allow same-sex marriages.

"(a) Resolution of the case depends
on whether petitioners were free as adults
to engage in private conduct in the exercise
of their liberty under the Due Process Clause.
For this inquiry the Court deems it necessary
to reconsider its *Bowers* holding. The *Bowers*
Court's initial substantive statement —'The
issue presented is whether the Federal Constitution
confers a fundamental right upon homosexuals
to engage in sodomy...,' 478 U.S. at 190 –
discloses the Court's failure to appreciate
the extent of the liberty at stake. To say
that the issue in Bowers was simply
the right to engage in certain sexual conduct
demeans the claim of the individual put
forward, just as it would demean a married
couple where it said that marriage is just
about the right to have sexual intercourse.
Although the laws involved in *Bowers* and here
purport to do not more than prohibit a
particular sexual act, their penalties and
purposes have more far-reaching consequences,

touching upon the most private human conduct,
sexual behavior, and in the most private of
places, the home. They seek to control a
personal relationship that, whether or not
entitled to formal recognition in the law,
is within the liberty of persons to choose
without being punished as criminals. The
liberty protected by the Constitution allows
homosexual persons the right to choose to
enter upon relationships in the confines
of their homes and their own private lives
and still retain their dignity as free persons.

(b) Having misapprehended the liberty
claim presented to it, the *Bowers* Court stated
that proscriptions against sodomy have ancient
roots. 478 U.S. at 192. It should be noted,
however, that there is no longstanding history
in this country of laws directed at homosexual
conduct as a distinct matter. Early American
sodomy laws were not directed at homosexuals
as such but instead sought to prohibit nonprocreative sexual activity more generally
whether between men and women or men and men.
Moreover, early sodomy laws seem not to have
been enforced against consenting adults acting
in private. Instead, sodomy prosecutions often
involved predatory acts against those who could
not or did not consent: relations between men
and minor girls or boys, between adults involving
force, between adults implicating disparity in
status, or between men and animals. The
longstanding criminal prohibition of homosexual
sodomy upon which *Bowers* placed such reliance is
as consistent with a general condemnation of

nonprocreative sex as it is with an established
tradition of prosecuting acts because of their
homosexual character. Far from possessing "ancient
roots," ibid., American laws targeting same-sex
couples did not develop until the last third
of the 20th century. Even now, only nine States
have singled out same-sex relations for criminal
prosecution. Thus, the historical grounds relied
upon in *Bowers* are more complex than the majority
opinion and the concurring opinion by Chief
Justice Burger there indicated. They are not
without doubt and, at the very least, are overstated.
The *Bowers* Court was, of course, making the
broader point that for centuries there have
been powerful voices to condemn homosexual
conduct as immoral, but this Court's obligation
is to define the liberty of all, not to mandate
its own moral code, *Planned Parenthood of
Southeastern Pa. v. Casey,* 505 U.S. 833, 850.
The Nation's laws and traditions in the past
half century are most relevant here. They
show an emerging awareness that liberty gives
substantial protection to adult persons in
deciding how to conduct their private
lives in matters pertaining to sex. See
County of Sacramento v. Lewis, 523 U.S. 833, 857.

(c) *Bowers'* deficiencies became even
more apparent in the years following its
announcement. The 25 States with laws
prohibiting the conduct referenced in *Bowers*
are reduced now to 13, of which 4 enforce
their laws only against homosexual conduct.
In those States, including Texas, that still
proscribe sodomy (whether for same-sex or

heterosexual conduct), there is a pattern of
nonenforcement with respect to consenting
adults acting in private. *Casey, supra,*[110] at
51 —which confirmed that the Due Process
Clause protects personal decisions relating to
marriage, procreation, contraception, family
relationships, child rearing, and education –
and *Romer v. Evans,* 517 U.S. 620, 624 —which
struck down class-based legislation directed
at homosexuals —cast *Bowers* into even
more doubt. The stigma the Texas criminal
statute imposes, moreover, is not trivial.
Although the offense is but a minor
misdemeanor, it remains a criminal offense
with all that imports for the dignity of
the persons charged, including notation of
convictions on their records and on job
application forms, and registration as sex
offenders under state law. Where a case's
foundations have sustained serious erosion,
criticism from other sources is of greater
significance. In the United States, criticism
of *Bowers* has been substantial and continuing,
disapproving of its reasoning in all respects,
not just to its historical assumptions. And,
to the extent *Bowers* relied on values shared
with a wider civilization, the case's reasoning
and holding have been rejected by the European
Court of Human Rights, and that other nations
have taken action consistent with an affirmation
of the protected right of homosexual adults to
engage in intimate, consensual conduct. There
has been no showing that in this country the
governmental interest in circumscribing personal
choice is somehow more legitimate or urgent.

Stare decisis[111] is not an inexorable command.
Payne v. Tennessee, 501 U.S. 808, 828. *Bowers'*
holding has not induced detrimental reliance
of the sort that could counsel against overturning
it once there are compelling reasons to do so.
Casey, supra, at 855-856. *Bowers* causes
uncertainty, for the precedents before and
after it contradicts its central holding. pp. 12-17.

(d) *Bowers* rationale does not withstand
careful analysis. In his dissenting opinion
in *Bowers* Justice Stevens concluded that (1)
the fact a State's governing majority has
traditionally viewed a particular practice as
immoral is not a sufficient reason for upholding
a law prohibiting the practice, and (2)
individual decisions concerning the intimacies of
physical relationships, even when not intended
to produce offspring, are a form of 'liberty'
protected by due process. That analysis should
have controlled *Bowers,* and it controls here.
Bowers was not correct when it was decided, is
not correct today, and is hereby overruled.
This case does not involve minors, persons
who might be injured or coerced, those who
might not easily refuse consent, or public
conduct or prostitution. It does involve
two adults who, with full and mutual consent,
engaged in sexual practices common to a
homosexual lifestyle. Petitioners' right
to liberty under the Due Process Clause
gives them the full right to engage in
private conduct without government intervention.
Casey, supra, at 847. The Texas statute
furthers no legitimate state interest which

can justify its intrusion into the individual's personal and private life. Pp. 17-18.

41 S.W. 3d 349, reversed and remanded."

Under the rule of *Stare decisis* the Bowers v. Hardwick[112] finding was binding case law on all courts in the nation. Some 17 years later, the Lawrence et al. v. Texas[113] case overturned Bowers stating that sodomy laws are unconstitutional. It is seldom that the United States Supreme Court reverses its own decision but, in this matter, it did. In doing so, the Court explained:

> "There has been no showing that in this country
> the governmental interest in circumscribing
> personal choice is somehow more legitimate or
> urgent. *Stare decisis* is not an inexorable
> command. *Payne v. Tennessee,* 501 U.S.808, 828.
> *Bowers'* holding has not induced detrimental
> reliance of the sort that could counsel against overturning
> it once there are compelling reasons
> to do so. *Casey, supra,* at 855-856. *Bowers*
> causes uncertainty, for the precedents before
> and after it contradicts its central holding."

The decision in Lawrence et al. v. Texas[114] was handed down and it became headline news throughout the media. The change in attitude and opinion of the Justices after seventeen years is noted. By the court holding that intimate consensual sexual conduct was part of the liberty protected by substantive due process under the Fourteenth Amendment the way was paved for a subsequent decision invalidating state laws prohibiting same-sex marriage. This raises the possibility of a challenge to the Defense of Marriage Act under the equal protection clause of the Fourteenth Amendment.

The extremely conservative religious-right successfully lob-bied the Congress and promoted an almost homophobic atti-tude among many legislators. The subject of blessing same-sex unions and ordaining gay clergy was circulating through many church bodies. This was clearly a threat to the agenda of the conservative political and religious right.

The Defense of Marriage Act[115] was enacted as federal law and is now the law of the land (subject to a constitutional chal-lenge).[116] After passing both the Senate and House it was signed into law by President Bill Clinton on September 21, 1996. The Act recites, in part, as follows:

"DEFENSE OF MARRIAGE ACT, 110 Stat. 2419
SECTION 1. SHORT TITLE.
The Act may be cited as the "Defense of Marriage Act".

SECTION 2. POWERS RESERVED TO THE STATES.
(a) IN GENERAL. CHAPTER 115 OF TITLE 28,
UNITED STATES CODE, IS AMENDED BY ADDING
AFTER SECTION 1738B THE FOLLOWING:

1738c. Certain acts, records, and proceedings
and the effect thereof.

No State, territory, or possession of the
United States, or Indian Tribe, shall be
required to give effect to any public act,
record, or judicial proceeding of any other
State, territory, possession, or tribe respecting
a relationship between persons of the same
sex that is treated as a marriage under the
laws of such other State, territory, possession,
or tribe, or a right or claim arising from such relationship.

SECTION 3. DEFINITION OF MARRIAGE.

(a) IN GENERAL. CHAPTER 1 OF TITLE 1, UNITED
STATES CODE, IS AMENDED BY ADDING AT THE
END THE FOLLOWING:
7. Definition of 'marriage' and 'spouse'
"In determining the meaning of any Act of
Congress, or of any ruling, regulation,
or interpretation of the various administra-
tive bureaus and agencies of the United
States, the word 'marriage' means only a
legal union between one man and one woman
as husband and wife, and the word 'spouse'
refers only to a person of the opposite sex
who is a husband or wife."[117]

At the time of this writing, this federal law is still considered "good law" because it has not been subjected to a constitutional challenge before the United States Supreme Court.

This law has barred same-sex marriages and has prevented
couples from receiving over a thousand rights[118], privileges and
entitlements that they would be entitled to if legally married.

The Federal Marriage Amendment is a proposal to amend
the Constitution of the United States. It would be the 28th
Amendment since 1791, and the only extant amendment to
constrict rather than expand civil rights.[119] The holding by the
Supreme Court in Lawrence et al. v. Texas caused a shockwave
in the religious and political right and urgency permeated the
proponents of the Defense of Marriage Act. The chance that
the Defense of Marriage Act would not survive a Constitutional challenge was a call to the proponents to take immediate
action.

The proposal to amend the Constitution with the Federal
Marriage Act was introduced into the House of Representatives on May 15, 2002, and again on May 21, 2003, by Repre-
sentative Marilyn Musgrave (R-Colorado), but the House has
not voted on it, as of the date of this writing.

The amendment proposed by Musgrave consists of two sentences:

"Marriage in the United States shall
consist only of the union of a man and a woman.
Neither this constitution or the constitution of any state, nor state or federal law,
shall be construed to require that marital
status or the legal incidents thereof be
conferred upon unmarried couples or groups."

The measure was introduced into the United States Senate and was debated. The measure went to a vote on July 14, 2004 and failed to gain the compulsory 60 votes to pass (Nays: 50, Yeas: 48, Not voting: 2.). It lost by 12 votes (a 2/3 majority vote is required in both houses of Congress to pass a constitutional amendment. The measure then must be ratified by a 2/3 majority of the States). President George W. Bush expressed his disappointment that the measure did not pass and pledged to push the matter forward. The political and religious right has vowed to continue their efforts to bring the matter up again in the next Congress.

In reading the two-sentence proposed Amendment, it becomes clear that the intent is to circumvent a constitutional challenge to the Defense of Marriage Act. The first sentence mandates that marriage shall consist of a union of a man and a man and woman. The second sentence is a requirement of compliance by the federal and all state constitutions to prevent same-sex marriages. It directly addresses the Full Faith and Credit clause of the U.S. Constitution.

Section one of Article Four of the United States Constitution is known as the "Full Faith and Credit Clause". It reads:

"Section 1. Full Faith and Credit
shall be given in each State to the public
Acts, Records, and judicial Proceedings of

every other State; And the Congress may by general Laws prescribe the Manner in which such Acts, Records and Proceedings shall be proved, and the Effect thereof."

If the Federal Marriage Amendment became an amendment to the constitution, there would be extreme chaos across the nation. As an example, some states recognize common law marriages, while other states do not. If a couple's marriage was recognized in one state as a legal marriage it would not require those states that do not have a common marriage law to recognize that marriage. Additionally, if a state recognized a same-sex marriage under their constitution, other states would not have to recognize it. The inclusion of this passage would prioritize judicial interpretation by implementing a different method by which federal and state anti-discrimination and equal protection laws guarantee interpretations for non-married couples, regardless of sexual orientation, are carried out. State laws include local city and county ordinances, codes and regulations. It would, in effect, give married couples constitutional protections that unmarried persons would not have. Married people today have a "favored status" with many entitlements but all people have equal protection under the Constitution.

Full faith and credit is practiced from the lowest to the highest courts on a daily basis and appeals courts in the various appellate court districts often make conflicting rulings on matters of law, which may stand in conflict until resolved by the U.S. Supreme Court or by legislative action. The Supreme Court of the United States has long recognized a "public policy exception" to the clause. When the legal pronouncements of one state have conflicted with the public policy of another state, federal courts in the past have been reluctant to force a state to enforce the pronouncements of another state in contravention of its own public policy. The public policy exception has been applied in case of marriage (such as polygamy, miscegenation or consanguinity), civil judgments and orders, criminal convictions and others.

The Full Faith and Credit clause has been noted for its application involving orders of protection, for which the clause was expounded upon by the Violence Against Women Act, child support, for which the enforcement of the clause was spelled out in the Federal Full Faith and Credit for Child Support Act, and its possible application to same-sex marriage, civil union and domestic partnership laws and cases, as well as the controversial Defense of Marriage Act and the proposed Federal Marriage Amendment. The clause has been the chief constitutional basis for the repeated attacks on the Defense of Marriage Act. Regardless of whether the Defense of Marriage Act is constitutional, most legal scholars recognize that it is more probably superfluous given the public policy exception. For even if the Defense of Marriage Act is deemed unconstitutional, the long precedence of the public policy exception weighs in against the recognition of same-sex marriage, civil unions, and domestic partnerships in states whose public policy prohibits it. As of early 2004, 39 states have passed their own laws nearly all of which specifically reject same-sex marriages recognized in other jurisdictions. Many of these laws have been passed in the last few years. By taking a legal stance on the issue these states have helped inform the Supreme Court what the public policy of the various states are before the Court takes up the issue and it is left to review the constitutionality of those policies.

Supreme Court Justice Antonin Scalia stated in his dissenting opinion to the landmark Lawrence v. Texas decision that he feared application of the full faith and credit clause to the majority's decision in that case might destroy "the structure...that has permitted a distinction to be made between heterosexual and homosexual unions." If Scalia's dissenting opinion held true, the majority ruling could potentially negate the Defense of Marriage Act and create a legal loophole allowing same-sex marriages and obliging all other states to recognize them.

Likewise, the Massachusetts Supreme Judicial Court case of Goodridge et al. v. Department of Public Health is being eyed by observers on both sides of the issue because of similar concerns stemming from this clause.

Supporters of the Defense of Marriage Act, however, have claimed that the clause could very well be used to defend the law. They say that the clause's explicit language spelling out the role for Congress is precisely what makes the law constitutional, with the further need for the Federal Marriage Amendment. They point out that Congress has made several laws, including those on firearms controls and safety standards, employment discrimination, disability, rights to unionization, and environmental protection, which have all withstood Constitutional attacks on the basis of full faith and credit.[120]

The proposed Federal Marriage Amendment would also affect rights guaranteed under other provisions of the Constitution. Consider the guarantee of equal protection under Section One of the Fourteenth Amendment to the Constitution:

"Section 1. All persons born or naturalized
in the United States and subject to the
jurisdiction thereof, are citizens of
the United States and of the State wherein
they reside. No State shall make or
enforce any law which shall abridge the
privileges or immunities of citizens of
the United States; nor shall any State
deprive any person of life, liberty, or
property, without due process of law;
nor deny to any person within its jurisdiction the equal protection of the laws."[121]

The equal protection clause is a part of the Fourteenth Amendment to the United States Constitution, which provides that "no state shall make or enforce any law which shall [...] deny to any person within its jurisdiction the equal protection of the laws."

The Fourteenth Amendment was enacted after the American Civil War to ensure free and equal treatment for ex-slaves (especially in Confederate States). Later interpretation imposed a general restraint on the government's power to discriminate against people on "classes" not only by race but also by sex, origin, illegitimacy, wealth and any other class. Some classes are treated as "protected classes," such as race, while laws regarding other classes are not subject to strict scrutiny. The equal protection clause was also interpreted as outlawing selective prosecution.

An unresolved and important legal issue to the Gay Rights Movement is the level of scrutiny the United States Supreme Court would apply to state and federal laws that prohibit same-sex unions.

To analyze if a law violates the equal protection clause, three questions need to be asked:

1.Does the law discriminate on the basis
of race? (Race is a protected class) If so,
apply "strict scrutiny": the law is unconstitutional unless it
is the least restrictive means of
serving a "compelling" government interest.

2.Does the law discriminate on the basis
of sex? If so, apply "intermediate scrutiny":
the law is unconstitutional unless it is
"substantially related" to an "important"
government interest.

3.Does the law discriminate on some other
basis? If so, apply the "rational basis
test": the law is unconstitutional unless
it is "reasonably related" to a "legitimate"
government interest.

The government would be hard-pressed to show that the Defense of Marriage Act protects any important government interest and, at the same time, circumvents the question of overt discrimination toward a significant class of Americans.[122]

Another relevant and important principle relates to Substantive Due Process.

Substantive Due Process is a fundamental constitutional legal theory upon which a privacy right is based. The doctrine of Substantive Due Process provides that the Due Process Clause not only requires due process (basic procedural rights), but it also protects basic substantive rights. Substantive rights are the rights that reserve to the individual the power to possess or to do certain things, despite the government's desire to the contrary. These are rights such as freedom of speech and religion. Procedural rights are special rights that dictate *how* the government can legally go about depriving a person's freedom or property or life, when the law otherwise gives it the power to do so.

The Due Process Clause of the Fifth Amendment reads:

"No person shall be ...deprived of life,
liberty, or property, without due process
of law; nor shall private property be taken
for public use without just compensation."

The Due Process Clause of the Fifth Amendment applies to the federal government. The Due Process Clause of Section 1 of the Fourteenth Amendment reads:

"...nor shall any State deprive any
person of life, liberty, or property,
without due process of law, nor deny to
any person within its jurisdiction the
equal protection of the laws."

Obviously, the Due Process Clause of Section 1 of the Fourteenth Amendment applies to the States. One case that had a profound impact in the rise of Substantive Due Process was Dred Scott v. Sanford.[123] In this case the Supreme Court held that a person's property right in his slaves cannot be extinguished simply by the act of moving to a free state. Even though Dred Scott was living in the "free" State of Wisconsin (then Territory), he was required to remain a slave. Because of this case, the Supreme Court began to realize that Due Process meant more than just procedure. Procedural Due Process gave the Court the power to say to the government, "You may not do this unless you do it in a certain way"; the Substantive Due Process allowed the Court to say, "You may not do this at all!"

Another theory of law relates to the Theories of Incorporation. Incorporation or absorption, in the opinion of Justice Cardozo, is a technique whereby the court imports the substantive rights contained in the first eight Amendments of the Constitution which otherwise apply only to the federal government, and makes those rights applicable to the states through the Fourteenth Amendment to the Constitution.[124] Selective Incorporation is a selective theory of natural rights. Those provisions that are implicit in the concept of ordered liberty will be applied to the states through the Fourteenth Amendment to the Constitution. This would mean that certain clauses of the Bill of Rights should be made applicable to the states, but not all. Justice Cardozo and Justice Frankfurter were both proponents of selective incorporation.

Under Substantive Due Process, the Supreme Court has developed a broader interpretation of the Clause, one that protects basic substantive rights, as well as the right to process. It holds that the Due Process Clauses of the Fifth and Fourteenth Amendments guarantee not only that appropriate and just procedures (the processes) be used whenever the government is punishing a person or otherwise taking away a person's life, freedom, or property, but that these clauses also guarantee that a person's life, freedom, and property cannot be taken without appropriate governmental justification, regardless of the procedures used to do the taking. In a sense, it makes the Due Process clause a Due Substance clause as well.

This is an extremely significant concept that greatly expands the power of judicial review exercised by the federal courts. This works in two ways:

1.It gives the federal courts unqualified
discretion to decide what substantive
rights are protected under Due Process
and how extensive that protection is.
This is done in two ways:

•Under the substantive aspect of the Incorporation doctrine, where the
Court adopts selected provisions of
the Bill of Rights and apply them to
the States under due Process. This
can be called Substantive Incorporation.

•Under the Fundamental Rights theory,
where the Court adopts whatever
substantive rights it thinks are so
basic, natural and fundamental that
they must be protected even without
reliance on any particular provision
of the Constitution. Instead, the Court
is said to root these guarantees directly
in the word Liberty in the Fourteenth Amendment's
Due Process Clause.

2.At the point when the federal courts
decide what substantive rights are

protected by Substantive Due Process, it
can use Judicial Review to enforce these
rights by reviewing all state legislation
for compliance with these rights.

As the law is now construed, a marriage (including a common-law marriage) in one state is universally recognized by all
other states.

Case law from the United States Supreme Court is quite
extensive on the subjects of Equal Protection and Full Faith
and Credit and Due Process.

On October 16, 2003, Rep. John Hostettler introduced
House Bill 3313, known as the "Marriage Protection Act", into
the House of Representatives. The bill would strip the U.S.
Supreme Court and all other federal courts of their jurisdiction to rule on challenges to state bans on same-sex marriages
under a provision of the 1996 Defense of Marriage Act. This
would effectively bar same-sex couples, who obtained a legal
marriage status in one state to have that marriage recognized in
other states. Following the huge defeat of the Federal Marriage
Amendment on Wednesday, July 21, 2003, and the threat to
the Defense of Marriage Act, the House Republicans brought
HR-3313 to the floor for a vote on Thursday, November 22,
2003, one day before the House and Senate would leave for a
six-week hiatus. The vote was along party lines and the measure passed on a 233-194 vote. The measure will now go to
the Senate where it is predicted it will not fare as well. The
non-partisan Congressional Research Service said it could find
no precedent for Congress passing a law to limit federal courts
from ruling on the constitutionality of a law.

While it could be fully expected that a constitutional challenge to the existing Defense of Marriage Act[125] would prevail,
it would not stop the current effort to obtain a constitutional
amendment to bar same-sex marriages. Because of the impact
of a multitude of laws and theories of laws, the matter of con-

sidering a same-sex marriage ban could be greatly convoluted.

The international community perceives the United States as a protector, defender and advocate for freedom, equality, and human rights. In recognition of the disenfranchisement of over 40 million Americans, it is held that the United States Constitution be amended to include a non-discrimination clause to ban discrimination on the basis of race, color, creed, sexual orientation, national origin/ethnicity and/or sex/gender. Such an action would nullify the Defense of Marriage Act and the Marriage Protection Act and provide the avenue for all Americans to share equally in the rights, privileges and benefits of our society, including that of marriage.

The Eighteenth Amendment to the Constitution enacted prohibition; the Twenty-first Amendment to the Constitution repealed the Eighteenth Amendment. The lesson learned is that one cannot legislate morality.

---

[94] Judgment in the U.S. Supreme Court Case Dred Scott v. John F. A. Sanford, March 7, 1857; Case Files 1792-1995; Record Group 267; Records of the Supreme Court of the United States, National Archives.

[95] The first federal act of forced desegregation came during World War II when President Truman desegregated the armed forces.

[96] This included segregation in public accommodations, housing, employment, etc.

[97] Harper v. Virginia State Board of Elections, 383 U.S. 663 (1966).

[98] South Carolina v. Katzenbach, 383 U.S. 302, 327-328 (1966. See also Allen v. State Board of Elections, 393 U.S. 544 (1969). It recognized that gerrymandered district boundaries or at-large elections could be used to dilute minority voting strength.

[99] White v. Regester, 412 U.S. 755 (1973).

[100] Mobile v. Bolden, 466 U.S. 55 (1980).

[101] White v. Regester, 412 U.S. 755 (1973).

[102] *"inter alia"* is a legal term meaning "among other things".

[103] Boy Scouts of America v. Dale (99-699) 530 U.S. 640 (2000).

[104] From a syllabus by the Reporter of Decisions of the U.S. Supreme Court.

[105] "id." (short for idem) is a legal term meaning "the same; used to indicate a reference previously made."

[106] "ex rel." (short for ex relatione) is a legal term meaning "upon relation or information".

[107] Bowers v. Hardwick 478 U.S. 186 (1986)

[108] Roger Nance was later cited for filing a false report and served 15 days in jail. Nance filed the report because of an ongoing "personality dispute" between him and Lawrence and Garner.

[109] Lawerence et al. v. Texas (02-102) 41 S.W. 3d 349).

[110] "supra" is a legal term that refers the reader to a previous part of the writing.

[111] "Stare decisis" is a legal term meaning "abiding by previous decisions".

[112] Bowers v. Hardwick, 478 U.S. 186 (1986).

[113] Lawrence and Garner v. Texas, Docket No. 02-0102 (U.S. Supreme Court).

[114] Ibid.

[115] Public Law 104-199, 100 Stat. 2419.

[116] While the Defense of Marriage Act is officially a federal law, most legal scholars believe it would not survive a Constitutional challenge. Many states have adopted the law as state law.

[117] Public Law 104-199, 100 Stat. 2419

[118] See Chapter I.

[119] The 18th Amendment, which banned alcohol in the United States, was completely repealed by the 21st Amendment.

[120] This discussion on the Full Faith and Credit clause very closely follows the discussion in Wikipedia, the free online encyclopedia.

[121] Constitution of the United States, Section 1 (in Congress: ratified July 9, 1868).

[122] This discussion of the Equal Protection Clause closely follows an article in Wikipedia, the free online encyclopedia.

[123] Dred Scott v. Sanford, 60 U.S. 393 (1857). See discussion of this case earlier in this chapter.

[124] See: Barron v. Baltimore, 32 U.S. (7 Pet.) 243 (1833).

[125] Public Law 104-199, 100 Stat. 2419

IV

EPILOGUE

*T*his writing is offered as a contribution toward a better understanding of some of the issues surrounding homosexuality, the Gay Movement for equal rights, and the subject of same-sex marriage. The basic premises of presenting this writing is that, as a result of misunderstanding, inherited negative attitudes and a form of religious and political persecution of homosexuals, a significant portion of our society has been, and is, disenfranchised. It is hoped that a degree of enlightenment might result from this writing. It is projected that, with enlightened attitudes, a new and heightened degree of tolerance toward and acceptance of homosexuals can be appreciated.

It is expected that an initial amount of apprehension might develop by some who are exposed to this writing since it will probably contradict certain prejudices. Boswell notes:

"The modern West appears to be in just
such a period of transition regarding various

groups distinguished sexually, and gay people
provide a particularly useful focus for the
study of the history of such attitudes. Since
they are still the objects of severe pro-
scriptive legislation, widespread public hostility,
and various civil restraints, all with ostensibly
religious justification, it is far easier to
elucidate the confusion of religion and
intolerance in their case than in that of
blacks, moneylenders, Jews, divorced persons,
or others whose status in society has so
completely ceased to be associated with religious
conviction that the correlation —even if
demonstrated at length —now seems limited,
tenuous, or accidental."[126]

The issue of homosexuality first began to intrigue scientists in the late nineteenth century. Most assumed that homosexual inclinations were congenital, and began debating between themselves whether it was a defect or a segment of the normal human sexual phenomena. This scientific inquiry eventually resulted in abandonment of these theories in favor of psychological explanations. In 1959 G. E. Hutchinson published a paper speculating on a genetic significance of "non-reproductive" sexuality (which he labeled "paraphilia"), including homosexuality.[127]

One unique theory developed in the 1970s generally labeled as the phobic theory of the origin of homosexuality[128] opined that gay people prefer sexual contact with their own gender because they are frightened of such contact with the opposite sex. This has largely been discredited by more current and modern research.

The scientific findings that homosexuality has a genetic basis was previously covered.

There appears to be a common notion that all homosexuals

are sexually active. This notion is no more true than saying all heterosexuals are sexually active. There are a great number of people (gay and straight) who, for whatever reason, choose not to be sexually active. Their sexual orientation may be either gay or straight, but their choice of being, or not being, sexually active is entirely a personal decision.

One of the questions probably raised by this writing is whether the ancient Christian ceremony of same-sex union (Holy Union) worked in the past as a "gay marriage ceremony." It most certainly did and is well documented. The fact that the ancient heterosexual marriage was devoid of romantic emotion at the time of the wedding and usually was only experienced later in the marriage seems unrealistic by today's standards where, apparently, the only factor leading to a marriage is an overwhelming romantic attraction. In the ancient world the only unions that were made because of romantic attraction were same-sex unions.

We are currently experiencing considerable political pressure originating from the extreme religious and political right to ban same-sex marriages and to prevent the courts from hearing any related case contending discrimination, due process, and/or equal protection. To allow such to occur would create chaos within our social, political, and legislative functioning that could permanently destroy the freedoms we now enjoy.

In our history there have been any number of movements by disenfranchised segments of our society that have resulted in Constitutional Amendments or federal laws granting those segments equal rights. The Eighteenth Amendment was ratified on January 16, 1919 and began prohibition until its repeal by the Twenty-First Amendment, which was ratified on December 5, 1933. It was conclusive that the effort of a nation to legislate morality would be doomed.

Conversely, those movements where protective legislation was adopted did survive, enforcing the position of the United States as a protector of human rights.

The international community perceives the United States as a protector, defender and advocate for freedom, equality, and human rights. Has the time not come for this nation to abandon prejudice, bias, bigotry and discrimination?

The Eighteenth Amendment to the Constitution enacted prohibition until its repeal by the Twenty-First Amendment to the Constitution. The lesson learned is that one cannot legislate morality.

---

[126] Boswell, John. **Christianity, Social Tolerance, and Homosexuality.** (Chicago and London: The University of Chicago Press, 1980).

[127] Hutchinson, G.W. **A Speculative Consideration of Certain Possible Forms of Sexual Selection in Man.** *American Naturalist* 93 (1959)

[128] Freund, Kurt, Ron Langevin, et al. **Phobic Theory of Male Homosexuality,** *Archives of Internal Medicine* 134 (1974). .

APPENDIX I

THE GILGAMESH EPIC

*T*his is a summary of the Gilgamesh Epic taken from a number of translations. It is the oldest known human writing dating to circa 2740 B.C. This summary concentrates on the Epic written on twelve stone tablets in cuneiform script (which means "wedge-shaped"). The fullest versions, from which this summary is made, was in the Akkadian language and was found in the ruins of the library of Ashurbanipal, king of Assyria from 669 to 663 B.C., at Nineveh. The library was destroyed by the Persians in 612 B.C., and all of the tablets were damaged in different degrees. Of specific interest to this writing is that the author actually signed his work as "Shin-eqi-unninni" —the earliest known human author. Some of the areas of missing lines are set forth in the Babylonian language translations. For the entire text of the Gilgamesh Epic, please see the translations by Maureen Gallery Kovacs[129] or by John Maier and John Gardner.[130]

The Epic was named for its hero, Gilgamesh, a tyrannical

Babylonian king who ruled the city of Uruk, known in the Bible as Erech (now Al Warka', Iraq). During this period a king ruled his own city according to any law he cared to make. The common lands shared between the "kingdoms" observed the Code of Hammurabi. The entire setting of this story occurs in the "Cradle of Civilization" near the Euphrates River in Iraq (then Babylonia). The city of Uruk was surrounded by a high masonry wall to ward off wild animals and to prevent invasion by other area kings. The position of king was attained by being the survivor of physical battle between any and all who wanted the position and who challenged the sitting king. In short, the king was the strongest person in the kingdom —the "king of the hill".

Gilgamesh built the city of Uruk and he was described as a huge, super powerful man with high intelligence. He was considered two-thirds god and one-third man. He was grossly arrogant and strutted through the city, lordly in his appearance. Gilgamesh was a young tyrant and treated his people harshly. He had an insatiable sexual appetite and any girl or boy or man or woman was fair game for him. As one account reads, "he left neither the son to the father nor the maid to her mother... the bride of the young man." He was the only person in the kingdom with the authority to marry couples. As such, he picked either the bride or the groom (or both) to share the wedding bed following the wedding celebration.

TABLET I

The oppressed people called out to the sky-god Anu, the chief deity of the city, to help them. Anu responded by sending a man with the strength of dozens of wild animals to serve as the subhuman rival to the superhuman Gilgamesh. Anu's creation was that of Enkidu who lived in the wild with the animals in the harsh and wild forest surrounding Gilgamesh's lands.

One of Gilgamesh's subjects, the son of a trapper, was

checking his traps in the forest and discovered Enkidu running naked with the wild animals and frolicking with them.

"He ate grasses with the gazelles, and
jostled at the watering hole with the animals;
as with animals his thirst was slaked with
(mere) water."

This confirmed what a notorious trapper had reported seeing first hand for three days in a row. The elders of the city went to the city gate and, while standing at the gate to the city, observed a naked wild man with the animals at the watering hole. The men of the city consulted together and, lest their children see such a sight, hired one of the temple harlots, Shamhat, with the instruction that when she encountered Enkidu, she was to sexually offer herself to him. The trapper contended that if Enkidu submitted to her, he would lose his strength and his wildness.

In the evening, near the watering hole, Shamhat sat naked waiting for the animals to come. When the animals came, Enkidu saw Shamhat and he submitted to her and instantly lost his strength and wildness, but gained understanding and knowledge.

"His lust groaned over her; for six days and
seven nights Enkidu stayed aroused, and had
intercourse with the harlot until he was sated
with her charms."

As he lamented for his lost state, Shamhat, the harlot, offered to take him into the city to show him Gilgamesh, the only man worthy of Enkidu's friendship and who could satisfy Gilgamesh's sexual appetite.

Meanwhile, Gilgamesh had two dreams. In the first, a huge meteorite fell to earth and was so great that Gilgamesh could not lift or turn it. The people of the city gathered around the meteorite and celebrated, and Gilgamesh embraced it. In the second dream, an axe appeared at Gilgamesh's door. It was so great that he could not lift or turn it. Gilgamesh asked his mother to explain the dreams and his mother, the goddess Rimat-Ninsun, told him a man of great strength and force would come to Uruk and Gilgamesh would embrace this man as he would a wife, and this man would help Gilgamesh perform great deeds.

Tablet 2

The city elders arranged for Enkidu to live with a group of shepherds who taught him how to tend flocks, eat, speak properly, and how to wear clothes. Once Enkidu was properly "civilized" he entered the city of Uruk during a great celebration. Gilgamesh had performed a marriage and was about to have sexual intercourse with the bride. Upon learning of Gilgamesh's intent, Enkidu became incensed and infuriated and he stood in the doorway, blocking Gilgamesh's way. They fought so furiously that the rafters shook and the walls rumbled. After some time, Gilgamesh won the upper hand and Enkidu conceded Gilgamesh's superiority. Each of the two stood in awe and appreciation of the other's strength and they embraced, kissed and became devoted friends. Enkidu moved in and lived with Gilgamesh and the two became the closest of couples. Gilgamesh's sexual appetite was fully satisfied and the people of Uruk were no longer harassed. Both of them lived the lazy life in the city and grew weak.

Gilgamesh conceived of a great adventure to journey to the great Cedar Forest in southern Iran and cut down all the trees. It would be necessary to kill Humbaba the Terrible, the great demon. Enkidu knew about Humbaba from his days of running wild in the forest and he attempted to convince Gilgamesh that such would be folly.

TABLET 3 (MOST OF THIS TABLET IS MISSING)

The city elders initially disagreed with Gilgamesh's planned adventure, but finally and reluctantly agreed. They entrusted the life of Gilgamesh in Enkidu's hands, who, the elders insist, should take the lead position in the battle with Humbaba. Gilgamesh's mother, the goddess Rimat-Ninsun prayed to the sun-god, Shamash, in fear of her son's great risk and asked the god why he put a restless heart in the breast of her son. Shamash assured her that he would guard Gilgamesh's life. Gilgamesh's mother commanded Enkidu to take the lead position in the battle with Humbaba and to guard Gilgamesh's life. Enkidu, now in near panic, again attempted to reason with Gilgamesh not to undertake the adventure, but Gilgamesh believeed he would succeed and planned to proceed.

TABLET 4

Gilgamesh and Enkidu set out on their journey to the Cedar Forest. Glilgamesh prayed daily to Shamash on each of the days during the six-day journey. Shamash responded to Gilgamesh's prayers in the form of dreams, and Enkidu interpreted the dreams. The first dream did not survive. In the second dream Gilgamesh saw himself wrestling a great bull that split the ground with his breath. Enkidu explained that the bull is the sun-god, Shamash, and he would protect Gilgamesh. In the third dream, Gilgamesh experienced the skies roaring with thunder and the earth heaving. Then came darkness and stillness, like death. Lightning flashed and struck the earth and fires flared. Death flooded from the skies. When the heat relented and the fires were out, the plains had turned to ash. Enkidu's interpretation is missing but it may be assumed that Enkidu related it in a positive light. The fourth dream is missing but Enkidu told Gilgamesh that he would be successful. The fifth dream is also missing.

When they reached the Cedar Forest, Gilgamesh was filled

with fear and prayed to Shamash, and reminded the sun-god that he [Shamash] promised his mother that he would be protected. Shamash called down to Gilgamesh telling him to enter the forest because Humbaba, who usually wore seven coats of armor, was now only wearing one, leaving him particularly vulnerable. Enkidu, however, lost his courage and began to return when Gilgamesh fell on him and they had a great fight. Hearing the noise of their fight, Humbaba came out of the Cedar Forest to challenge Gilgamesh and Enkidu. Much of the tablet is missing here but the remaining remnant tells of Gilgamesh convincing Enkidu to stand together in facing the demon, Humbaba.

TABLET 5

Gilgamesh and Enkidu entered the lush Cedar Forest and started cutting down the trees. Humbaba heard the sound and came before them, warning them off. Enkidu told Humbaba that the two of them were much stronger than the demon. Humbaba knew that Gilgamesh was a king and taunted the king for taking orders from Enkidu. Humbaba turned his face into a ferocious mask and began to threaten Gilgamesh and Enkidu. Gilgamesh ran away and hid. Enkidu shouted inspiration and courage to Gilgamesh and he came out from hiding; the two began their epic battle with Humbaba. During the battle, the sun-god, Shamash, intervened and helped the duo defeat Humbaba. Humbaba was on his knees with Gilgamesh's sword at his throat and he begged for his life, offering Gilgamesh the entire forest and his eternal servitude. While thinking this over, Enkidu told Gilgamesh to kill Humbaba before other gods arrived and prevented him from doing so. Enkidu reminded Gilgamesh that by killing Humbaba he would gain widespread fame forever. Gilgamesh, with a wide sweep of his sword, beheaded Humbaba but, before he died, Humbaba screamed a curse on Enkidu:

"Of you two, may Enkidu not live the longer,
may Enkidu not find any peace in this world."

Gilgamesh and Enkidu resumed their effort of cutting
down all of the trees in the Cedar Forest and they selected the
tallest to bring back to Uruk to construct a great cedar gate at
the entrance to the city. They built a raft out of some of the
cedars and floated down the Euphrates River to Uruk.

TABLE 6

After arriving in Uruk, Gilgamesh's fame spread wide and
far. Wearing his finest clothes he attracted the sexual attention
of the goddess, Ishtar, who offered to be his lover. Gilgamesh
rebukeds Ishtar with insults, noting all the mortal lovers that
Ishtar had had, and the dire ends they met at her hands. Ishtar,
deeply insulted, returned to her father in heaven, the sky-god
Anu, and asked to let her have the Bull of Heaven to wreak
vengeance on Gilgamesh and Uruk. She explained her need
for the Bull of Heaven to kill Gilgamesh and the people of
Uruk. Ishtar threatened that, if her request was not granted,
she would pull down the Gates of Hell, crush the doorposts,
flatten the door, and allow the dead to leave hell and roam the
earth where they would eat the living, and death would then
overwhelm all the living. Anu gave her the Bull of Heaven and
he was sent down into Uruk. When he breathed, enormous
abysses were opened in the earth and hundreds of people fell
into them to their certain deaths. Gilgamesh and Enkidu, as a
team, slew the mighty bull and enraged Ishtar. Enkidu insulted
her and told her that she was next in line and he and Gilgamesh
would kill her next. He then ripped one of the thighs off the
bull and hurled it into her face.

TABLET 7

Enkidu had a series of dreams, became weak and then ill.

He summoned the priests, who informed him that he had been singled out by the gods for vengeance. He was informed that the chief gods concluded between them that someone should be held responsible and punished for the death of Humbaba and the Bull of Heaven. Between Gilgamesh and Enkidu, the gods decided that the penalty should fall to Enkidu. Enkidu became angry and enraged and he cursed the Cedar Gate they built from the wood of the Cedar Forest, and he cursed Shamhat, the harlot, and the trapper for finding him in the forest and introducing him to civilization. Shamhat reminded him that, even though he had a short life, he enjoyed the blessings of civilization and great happiness. Enkidu reconsidered his lot and then blessed the harlot and the trapper. In a dream, a great demon ensnared Enkidu and pulled him to Hell, a House of Dust where all the dead go and, as he was dying, Enkidu described Hell:

> "The house where the dead dwell in total darkness,
> Where they drink dirt and eat stone,
> Where they wear feathers like birds,
> Where no light ever invades their everlasting darkness,
> Where the door and the lock of Hell is coated with
> thick dust.
> When I entered the House of Dust,
> On every side the crowns of kings were heaped,
> On every side the voices of the kings who wore those
> crowns,
> Who now only served food to the gods Anu and Enlil,
> Candy, meat, and water poured from skins.
> I saw sitting in this House of Dust a priest and a servant,
> I also saw a priest of purification and a priest of ecstasy,
> I saw all the priests of the great gods.
> There sat Etana and Sumukan,
> There sat Ereshkigal, the queen of Hell,
> Beletseri, the scribe of Hell, sitting before her.

Beletseri held a tablet and read it to Ereshkigal.
She slowly raised her head when she noticed me.
She pointed at me:
'Who has sent this man?'"

Enkidu commended himself to his dear friend and lover, Gilgamesh, and, after suffering for twelve days, died.[131]

TABLET 8

Gilgamesh held Enkidu's still body on his lap for days until it turned to clay. Gilgamesh was devastated by the death of his dear friend, lover, and companion and, during a long lament, ordered all of creation to remain silent while he mourned his beloved Enkidu. Much of this tablet is missing but the last half appears to describe a beautiful monument Gilgamesh built for Enkidu.

TABLE 9

After Enkidu's death, Gilgamesh realized that someday he too would die, and he went into a panic and allowed his life to fall apart. He discontinued bathing and shaving and caring for himself. He finally came to a conclusion that he couldn't live unless he was granted eternal life; he decided to go on the most risky journey of all —a journey to Utnapishtim and to Utnapishtim's wife, who were the only mortals preserved by the gods during the Great Flood.[132]

After a deep dream, Gilgamesh set out on his journey and finally arrived at Mount Mashu. Mount Mashu guarded the rising and the setting of the sun, and he met the two huge scorpions guarding the way past Mount Mashu. The scorpions attempted to convince Gilgamesh that his journey was useless, risky, and dangerous, but they allowed him to pass. Past Mount Mashu was considered the land of Night, where light was absent. Gilgamesh traveled eleven leagues before he again emerged into the light of day. He entered into a beautiful garden of gleaming gems where every tree and bush bore precious stones.

Tablet 10

Gilgamesh continued his journey and came upon a tavern on a shore near the ocean that was owned by Siduri. Siduri saw Gilgamesh coming and was apprehensive because of his disheveled appearance. She locked the door to the tavern and refused to let Gilgamesh in. After Gilgamesh proved his identity he inquired about directions to Utnapishtim. She told him the journey was extremely risky and directed him to Urshanabi, a ferryman who was employed by Utnapishtim. Gilgamesh introduced himself to Urshanabi with great arrogance and violence, ruining the "stone things" that were required for the trip to Utnapishtim, and demanding that the ferryman take him to Utnapishtim. The ferryman informed Gilgamesh that after destroying the "stone things" the trip was impossible. The ferryman told Gilgamesh to cut down several trees to be used as punting poles. He informed Gilgamesh that he must cross the Waters of Death where any mortal who touched the water would die instantly. With the poles he could push the boat without coming into contact with the dangerous waters.

Gilgamesh set out on the dangerous journey and eventually arrived at another shore and met a man, informing him that he was looking for Utnapishtim and the secret of eternal life. The old man informed Gilgamesh that death was necessary and was the will of the gods —human life was only temporary and not permanent.

Tablet 11

A realization crept over Gilgamesh that he was actually talking to Utnapishtim, the Far-Away. He didn't expect an immortal human man to be so ordinary appearing or to be so old. He inquired of Utnapishtim how he was able to attain immortality and Utnapishtim informed him of the great secret that was hidden from humans. He explained that in the time before the Flood, there was a city called Shuruppak on the banks of the Euphrates. It was there that the council of the gods held a secret meeting and resolved to destroy the world in a great flood. All the gods swore an oath to keep the secret from all humans. One of the gods that created humanity, Ea, came to Utnapishtim's house and told the secret to the walls of Utnapishtim's house—to build a great boat, its length as great as its breadth, to cover the boat, and to bring all living things into the boat. Utnapishtim went straight to work and finished the great boat by the new year. Utnapishtim loaded the boat with gold, silver, and all the living things of the earth and then he launched the boat. Ea ordered him into the boat and to close the door behind him. Thick black clouds gathered with the thunder god, Adad, rumbling with them. The earth split like an earthenware pot, and the light turned to darkness. The flood grew so great that it scared the gods.

The gods shook like beaten dogs, hiding in the far corners of heaven.

Ishtar screamed and wailed:

"The days of old have turned to stone:
We have decided evil things in our Assembly!
Why did we decide those evil things in our Assembly?
We have only just now created our beloved humans;
We now destroy them in the sea!"
All the gods wept and wailed along with her,
All the gods sat trembling, and wept.

After seven days and seven nights the flood subsided and light returned to the earth. Utnapishtim opened a window and the entire world had been turned into a flat ocean; all human beings had been turned to stone and Utnapishtim fell to his knees and wept.

Finally, Utnapishtim's boat came to rest on top of Mount Nimush and lodged firmly on the peak of the mountain, with the bottom of the hull just below the surface of the ocean, remaining there for seven days. On the seventh day, Utnapishtim related:

> "I released a dove from the boat,
> It flew off, but circled around and returned,
> For it could find no perch.
> I then released a swallow from the boat,
> It flew off, but circled around and returned,
> For it could find no perch.
> I then released a raven from the boat,
> It flew off, and the waters had receded:
> It eats, it scratches the ground, but it does not
> circle around and return.
> I then sent out all the living things in every direction
> and sacrificed a sheep on that very spot."

The gods detected the odor of the sacrificed sheep and gathered around Utnapishtim. The god who originally proposed to kill all humans, Enlil, arrived and became furious to learn that one of the humans had survived. Enlil accused Ea of breaking his sworn oath and Ea convinced Enlil to be merciful to him. Enlil then seized Utnapishtim and his wife and blessed them:

> "At one time Utnapishtim was mortal.
> At this time let him be a god and immortal;
> Let him live in the Far Away at the source of all
> the rivers."

Having finished his explanation, Utnapishtim suggested that Gilgamesh could also gain immortality if he could stay awake for six days and seven nights. Gilgamesh accepted the suggestion and sat down on the shore, instantly falling asleep. Utnapishtim informed his wife that all humans are liars, and that Gilgamesh would deny that he fell asleep. He instructed his wife to bake a loaf of bread every day and lay the loaf at Gilgamesh's feet. Gilgamesh slept for six days and seven nights without waking. Utnapishtim woke him up and the surprised Gilgamesh retorted, "I only just dozed off for half a second here." Utnapishtim showed Gilgamesh the loaves of bread and their state of decay from the most recent, fresh bread to the oldest, moldy and stale bread. Gilgamesh lamented:

"O woe! What do I do now, where do I go now?
Death has devoured my body,
Death dwells in my body,
Wherever I go, wherever I look, there stands
Death!"

Utnapishtim's wife convinced the old man to show mercy to Gilgamesh. Utnapishtim, instead of offering immortality, offered Gilgamesh a secret plant that would make him young again. The plant was at the bottom of the ocean surrounding the Far-Away. Gilgamesh tied rocks to his feet and sank to the bottom of the ocean and picked the magic plant. However, Gilgamesh didn't trust the plant and he didn't use it. He decided to bring it back to Uruk and test it out on an old man first, just to make sure it worked.

Urshanabi took Gilgamesh across the Waters of Death. They traveled several leagues inland where they stopped to eat and sleep. While they were sleeping, a snaked slithered into their camp and ate the plant (which is why they shed their skins and crawl away). Gilgamesh woke and found the plant gone and he fell to his knees and lamented:

"For whom have I labored?
For whom have I journeyed?

For whom have I suffered?
I have gained absolutely nothing for myself,
I have only profited the snake, the ground lion!"

At the conclusion of the Epic, Gilgamesh stood at the gates of Uruk and invited Urshanabi to tour the city and to realize its greatness. He pointed out the high walls, its masonwork and, at the base of its gates, at the foundation of the city walls, where a lapis lazuli stone was situated, upon which was carved Gilgamesh's account of his experiences.

Tablet 12

The translator eliminated Tablet 12 for personal reasons, with support from many literary, archaeological, and linguistic experts as it appears to be somewhat of a sequel of the first eleven tablets, and depicts a story of Enkidu retrieving objects that Gilgamesh dropped in hell.

---

[129] Gallery Kovacs, Maureen. **The Epic of Gilgamesh.** (Stanford: Stanford University Press, 1990).

[130] Maier, John and John Gardner. **Gilgamesh.** (New York: Vintage Press, 1981).

[131] The comparison in the relationship between Gilgamesh and Enkidu in the Epic and the relationship between Johnathan and David in the Bible are striking.

[132] Some scholars believe that Utnapishtim was, in reality, the great-grandson of Noah.

APPENDIX II

EXAMPLES OF CEREMONIES
for
THE BLESSING OF
SAME-SEX UNIONS

*F*ollowing an extensive search in the major archives of Europe, John Boswell found some very ancient liturgies or ceremonies for the blessing of same and opposite sex unions. Unfortunately, most were in Greek as none of the Latin survived. The following is his introduction to this section of his work.

> "Although translation of ancient religious
> texts into premodern rather than contemporary
> English is likely to strike many readers as
> precious, I have elected to do so after carefully
> deliberating the problem—and discussing it
> with other scholars —for many years. The Greek

and Slavic in which these texts were written
was not the ordinary vernacular of the persons
who composed or subsequently utilized the
ceremonies; they were special, learned,
liturgical languages rooted consciously in the
much older speech patterns of Koine Greek and
Old Church Slavonic, used specifically for
Sacred Scripture and ecclesiastical functions,
with characteristic and peculiar cadence,
grammar, and vocabulary, imparting force, beauty,
and authority. Modern English translations of
Scripture and prayers into the modern vernacular
meet with resistance on the part of many of the
faithful. I take no side in this controversy,
which pits the advantages of accessibility and
relevance against the aesthetics and authority
of tradition."[133]

I have chosen to reprint a small number of these ceremonies as examples for the interested reader. For a fuller collection of these translations please consult Boswell.[134]

"Belgrade"[135]

[date uncertain; before the eighteenth century]
[Serbian Slavonic]

National Library of Belgrade

The Order of Celebrating the Union of Two Men

I.

The priest shall place the right hand of the elder upon the holy Gospel and upon that of the younger.

Then: Blessed be God, now and for ever and ever. Amen.

Holy God, holy mighty, holy immortal, have mercy upon us.

Most Holy Trinity, have mercy upon us.

O Lord, forgive us our sins.

O Ruler, pardon our wrongdoings.

O Holy one, look down and attend to our weakness for thy name's sake.

II.

Our Father who art in heaven, hallowed be thy name. Thy kingdom come. Thy will be done, on earth as it is in heaven. Give us this day our daily bread, and forgive us our trespasses, as we forgive those who trespass against us. And lead us not into temptation, but deliver us from evil. Amen.

For thine is the kingdom and the power and the glory.

III.

Hymn of the church or of the day, in the first tone.

Oh Lord, rescue thy people.

IV.

Then shall the priest take the holy belt and tie it around them. And they that are to be joined shall hold the holy belt in their left hands.

V.

(*First prayer*) Let us pray.

O Lord, Our God, who hast vouchsafed unto us the promise of salvation, and hast commanded us to love one another and to forgive one another our trespasses, Thou art the Author of grace and Friend of mankind, accept Thou these two servants, N. and N., who love each other with a love of the spirit, and have desired to come into thy holy church, and grant unto them hope, unashamed faithfulness, and true love. As Thou didst bestow upon thy holy disciples and apostles peace and love, grant these also the same, O Christ our Lord, and vouchsafe unto them every promise of salvation and life everlasting. For to Thee do we give glory, [Father and Son.]

VI.

(Second prayer) Lord God almighty, who didst fashion humankind after thine image and likeness and bestow upon us eternal life, Thou thoughtest it right that thy holy and glorious apostles Peter and Paul, and Philip and Bartholomew, should be joined together in perfect love, faith, and love of the heart. Thou also didst deem it proper for the holy martyrs Serge and Bacchus to be united. Bless Thou these thy servants. Grant unto them grace and prosperity, and faith and love; let them love each other without envy and without temptation all the days of their lives, through the power of the Holy Spirit and the prayers of our Holy Queen, the Mother of God and ever-virgin Mary, and all thy saints, who worship Thee through the ages.

For thine is the power and thine the kingdom, Father, Son and Holy Spirit, now and for ever and ever.

VII.

The deacon:
In unity we beseech Thee, O Lord.
For heavenly peace.
For the salvation of our souls, we beseech Thee, O Lord.
For the peace of the whole world.
For the prosperity of the holy churches of God and all they that are come together [in them], we beseech Thee, O Lord.
For them that are come together in the pledge of lifelong love, we beseech Thee, O Lord.
For these thy servants [and] for their being joined unto each other, we beseech Thee, O Lord.

That the Lord our God unite them in perfect love and inseparable life, we beseech Thee, O Lord.

That He grant them wisdom and true love, we beseech Thee, O Lord.

For the presanctified gift of the precious Body and Blood of our Lord Jesus Christ, that they receive it without sin and that it preserve their union without envy, we beseech Thee, O Lord.

That he grant them every promise for salvation, we beseech Thee, O Lord.

That he free us from all sorrow, anger and affliction, we beseech Thee, O Lord.

Protect, save, have mercy on and protect [them], O Lord, by the most holy, perfect and blessed grace.

VIII.

(Tropanion in the third tone) I will tell the names of the brethren.

(Verse) Serve the Lord with fear, and rejoice [with trembling].

IX.

[The First Epistle of] the Apostle Paul to the Corinthians [12:27-31]:

Now ye are the body of Christ, and members in particular. And God hath set some in the church, first apostles, secondarily prophets, thirdly teachers, after that miracles, then gifts of healings, helps, governments, diversities of tongues. Are all apostles? are all prophets?

Are all teachers? are all workers of miracles? Have all the gifts of healing? do all speak with tongues? do all interpret? But covet earnestly the best gifts: and yet shew I unto you a more excellent way. Though I speak with the tongues of men and of angels, and have not love, I am become as sounding brass, or a tinkling cymbal.

And though I have the gift of prophecy, and understand all mysteries, and all knowledge, and though I have faith, so that I could remove mountains, and have not love, I am nothing. And though I bestow all my goods to feed the poor, and though I give my body to be burned, and have not love, it profiteth me nothing.

Love suffereth long, and is kind; love envieth not; love vaunteth not itself, is not puffed up.

Doth not behave itself unseemly, seeketh not her own, is not easily provoked, thinketh no evil;

Rejoiceth not in iniquity, but rejoiceth in the truth;

Beareth all things, believeth all things, hopeth all things, endureth all things.

Love never faileth.

x.

Alleluia.

Behold, how good and how pleasant it is for brethren to dwell together in unity.

The Gospel according to John [17:1, 18-26]:

At that time, Jesus lifted up his eyes to his disciples, and prayed, As thou hast sent me into the world, [Father,] even so have I also sent them into the world.

And for their sakes I sanctify myself, that they also might be sanctified through the truth.

Neither pray I for these alone, but for them also which shall believe in me through their word.

That they all may be one, as thou, Father, art in me, and I in thee, that they also may be one in us: that the world may believe that thou has sent me.

And the glory which thou gavest me I have given them;

that they may be one, even as we are one:

I in them, and thou in me, that they may be made perfect in one; and that the world may know that thou hast sent me, and hast loved them, as thou hast loved me.

Father, I will that they also, whom thou has given me, be with me where I am; that they may behold my glory, which thou hast given me: for thou lovedst me before the foundation of the world.

O righteous Father, the world hath not known thee: but I have known thee, and these have known that thou hast sent me.

And I have declared unto them thy name, and will declare it: that the love wherewith thou hast loved me may be in them, and I in them.

XI.

Then: Peace be with you.
Then shall the priest kiss them.
And the two that are to be joined shall kiss each other.

XII.

The priest: Peace be with you.
The people: And with thy spirit.
[The priest:] Let us bow our heads.
The first prayer in a low voice:

O Lord our God, Thou art Author of love, teacher of grace and savior of all, grant unto us thy servants true love to think on Christ Jesus, thine only Son. And vouchsafe unto us to serve Thee and to live according to the laws of thy Christ, with our whole hearts.

Aloud: For thine is all glory and honor.

And then: Grant, O Lord, that we may worthily call upon thee with perfect earnestness, O heavenly God, our Father.

XIII.

The people: Our Father, who art in heaven, hallowed be thy name. Thy kingdom come. Thy will be done, on earth as it is in heaven. Give us this day our daily bread, and forgive us our trespasses, as we forgive those who trespass against us. And lead us not into temptation, but deliver us from evil. For thine is the kingdom, the power [and the glory].

XIV.

Then shall the priest elevate the bread, [saying], Behold the holy for the holy.
The people: Thou only art holy, Thou only art Lord, O Jesus Christ, in the glory of God the Father. Amen.
And he shall give them Communion if they be meet partakers thereof. If not…, he gives them kisses, bread and wine.

XV.

After the Communion, he shall place a cross in the sanctuary and lead them around it. Then they shall bow three times. Then shall the priest sing with them,
Turn thee again, Thou God of hosts, look down from heaven, behold and visit this vine; And the place of the vineyard that thy right hand hath planted.

XVI.

Three times in the sixth tone: Glory to Thee, O Christ, God, praise to Apostles and joy to martyrs and to them that preach the consubstantial Trinity, One in being, Holy martyrs who performed good works and are crowned with heavenly crowns, pray to the Lord that He save our souls.

XVII.

Holy, equally worthy of praise, most holy Virgin, with the prayers of the prophets and martyrs, priests, apostles, pray with the Mother of God for the salvation of our souls.

XVIII.

(Verse) Blessed are they that fear God.

(Verse) Behold, how good and how pleasant it is for brethren to dwell together in unity.

(Chant, litany) Have mercy upon us, O God, for thy great kindness. Lord, hear us and have mercy. Lord, have mercy. *(Three times.)*

XIX.

We pray further for these servants, N. and N., for their life, their health, their salvation and forgiveness of their sins. May they continue in union without blame and without temptation. Let us all say: Lord have mercy. *(Thirty times.)*

XX.

And the rest.
And he shall dismiss them.

GROTTAFERRATA I₁[136]

[Eleventh century] [Greek]

OFFICE FOR SAME-SEX UNION

I.

The priest shall place the holy Gospel on the Gospel stand and they that are to be joined together place their (right) hands on it, holding lighted candles in their left hands. Then shall the priest cense them and say the following:

II

In peace we beseech Thee, O Lord.

For heavenly peace, we beseech Thee, O Lord.

For the peace of the entire world, we beseech Thee, O Lord.

For this holy place, we beseech Thee, O Lord.

That these thy servants, N. and N., be sanctified with thy spiritual benediction, we beseech Thee, O Lord.

That their love abide without offense or scandal all the days of their lives, we beseech Thee, O Lord.

That they be granted all things needed for salvation and godly enjoyment of life everlasting, we beseech Thee, O Lord.

That the Lord God grant unto them unashamed faithfulness (and) sincere love, we beseech Thee, O Lord.

That we be saved, we beseech Thee, O Lord.

Have mercy on us, O God.

"Lord, have mercy" shall be said three times.

III

The priest (shall say)

Forasmuch as Thou, O Lord and Ruler, are merciful and loving, didst establish humankind after thine image and likeness, who didst deem it meet that thy holy apostles Philip and Bartholomew be united, bound one unto the other not by nature but by faith and the spirit. As Thou didst find thy holy martyrs Serge and Bacchus worthy to be united together, bless also these thy servants, N. and N., joined together not by the bond of nature but by faith and in the mode of the spirit, granting unto them peace and love and oneness of mind. Cleanse from their hearts every stain and impurity, and vouchsafe unto them to love one another without hatred and without scandal all the days of their lives, with the aid of the Mother of God and all thy saints, forasmuch as all glory is thine.

SINAI EUCHOLOGION[137]

[Eleventh —twelfth century —Old Church Slavonic]
[From Macedonia, but written in Old Church Slavonic with Glagolitic characters)

THE ORDER OF UNITING TWO MEN

Placing them before the altar, the deacon shall say these decanal prayers:
In peace, we pray to the Lord.
For heavenly [peace].
For the peace of all
For their joining together in union of love and life, we pray to the Lord.
For these servants of God, _____ and _____, and for their union in Christ, we pray to the Lord.
That the Lord our God unite them in perfect love and inseparable life, we pray to the Lord.
That they be granted discretion and sincere love, we pray to the Lord.
For the presanctified gift of the precious body and blood of our Lord Jesus Christ, that they should receive it without sin and preserve their union without envy, we pray to the Lord
That they and we be granted all things necessary for salvation, we pray to the Lord.
That they and we be preserved from all suffering, danger and need.
Protect, save.
Most holy, most pure.

PRAYER FOR SAME-SEX UNION

O Lord our God, who grant us what we ask for our salvation, who hath commanded us to love each other and to pardon each other [our] transgressions, bless, Lord, giver of good [things], love of mankind, these two servants of thine who love each other with a love of the spirit and have come to thy holy temple wishing to receive thy sanctification and benediction; grant them unabashed faithfulness and sincere love, and just as you gave thy holy disciples and apostles peace and love, grant [them] also to these, Christ our God, giving them all those things necessary for salvation and eternal life.

(*Exclamation*) For Thou art the light of truth and eternal life, and to Thee we give glory and praise, Father and Son and [Holy Spirit].

III. *Then prayeth the deacon:*

Let us hear the wisdom of the holy Gospel.
The priest readeth from John [17:1, 18-26]:

Jesus lifted up his eyes and said "Father, ...

as thou has sent me into the world, even so have I also sent them into the world.

And for their sakes I sanctify myself, that they also might be sanctified through the truth.

Neither pray I for these alone, but for them also which shall believe in me through their word;

That they all may be one; as thou, Father, are in me, and I in thee, that they also may be one in us: that the world may believe that thou has sent me.

And the glory which thou gavest me I have given them; that they may be one, even as we are one:

I in them, and thou in me, that they may be made perfect in one; and that the world may know that thou has sent me, and hast loved them, as thou hast loved me.

Father, I will that they also, whom thou hast given me, be with me where I am; that they may behold my glory, which thou has given me: for thou lovedst me before the foundation of the world.

O righteous Father, the world hath not known thee: but I have known thee, and these have known that thou hast sent me.

And I have declared unto them thy name, and will declare it: that the love wherewith thou hast loved me may be in them, and I in them.

It is to be found on the seventh Sunday after Easter. And when the priest finisheth the Gospel, the deacon shall recite the decanal prayers.

IV.

The priest shall make this prayer before the table:
Lord God omnipotent, who didst fashion humankind after thine image and likeness and gavest unto them life eternal, whom it hath pleased that thy holy and glorious apostles Peter and Paul, and Philip and Bartholomew, be joined together not by the bond of blood but of fidelity and love, who didst deem it meet for the holy martyrs Serge and Bacchus to be united together, bless Thou also these thy servants N. and N., joined together not of birth, but of faith and love. Grant unto them to love one another, let them continue without envy and without temptation all the days of their lives, through the power of thy Holy Spirit and the prayers of the Holy Mother of God and all thy saints who have pleased Thee throughout the ages.

(Exclamation) For thine is the power and thine the kingdom, thine the strength [and the glory. In the name of the Father, the Son and the Holy Spirit, now and forever. Amen.]

V.

The priest shall raise his voice and pray: Peace to all.
The deacon: Let us love one another.

Then shall the priest kiss the pair and they one another. Then the deacon shall pray: Let us bow our head before the Lord.

VI.

And the priest shall make this prayer in a low voice:
O Lord our God, thou art the author of love, the master of peace, and the savior of all, vouchsafe unto us thy love, the fulfillment of the law, and grant unto us to think on that which is of Jesus, thine only Son, our God. Vouchsafe us to receive one another with love, as thine only son did receive us, and grant unto us to serve one another in love and most heartily to fulfill the law of thy Christ.

(Exclmation) For thine is the glory and the power, Father, Son [and Holy Spirit].

VII.

And then shall the priest pray, raising up his arms:
And grant unto us, O Lord, earnestly to serve Thee.
The people: Our father, [who are in heaven, hallowed be thy name. Thy kingdom come. Thy will be done, on earth as it is in heaven. Give us this day our daily bread, and forgive us our trespasses, as we forgive those who trespass against us. And lead us not into temptation, but deliver us from evil. Amen.] *(To the end.}*

(Exclamation) For thine is the kingdom, the power and [the glory].

VIII.

And then [the deacon] shall say:
Behold the holy for the holy.
And the priest, lifting up the ciborium, shall say:
Behold the presanctified holy of holies.
The people: Thou only art holy, O Lord, Jesus Christ.
And he shall give Communion to both.

IX.

And after they have communicated the priest shall take the elder of them that have been joined together and the latter of them in turn takes the younger by the hand, and [the priest] leadeth them both, chanting the eighth tone of David.

Lord, [lead me] in [thy] truth.

Turn thee again, Thou God of hosts, look down from heaven, behold and visit this vine; And the place of the vineyard that thy right hath planted....

(*Verse*) Blessed is the man that feareth the Lord, that delighteth greatly in his commandments.

Lord, Lord, look down from heaven.

(*Verse*) Give ear, O Shepherd of Israel, thou that leadest [Joseph like a flock].

X.

(*Verse*) [Behold,] how good and how pleasant it is for brethren to dwell together in union.

It is like the precious ointment upon the head, that ran down upon the beard, even Aaron's beard: that went down to the skirts of his garments; As the dew of Hermon, and as the dew that descended upon the mountains of Zion: for there the Lord commanded the benediction, even life for evermore.]

And thus singing this whole psalm, verse by verse, unto the end, they shall add this verse:

Lord, Lord, look down from heaven ...

XI.

Then shall they sing the hymn of the martyrs, following the tone.

XII.

And then: Glory be to the Father, and to the Son: and to the Holy Spirit. As it was in the beginning, is now, and ever shall be: world without end. Amen.

XIII.

And the hymn to the Mother of God.

---

[133] Boswell, John. **Same-Sex Unions in Premodern Europe.** *Appendix of Translations.* (New York, Villard Books, 1994).

[134] Ibid.

[135] Ibid.

[136] Ibid.

[137] Ibid.

www.ingramcontent.com/pod-product-compliance
Lightning Source LLC
Chambersburg PA
CBHW051426280526
45785CB00003B/1180